net.speak
the
internet
dictionary

net.speak

the

internet

dictionary

Tom Fahey
Edited by Ruffin Prevost

Hayden
Books

net.speak—the internet dictionary

©1994 Hayden Books, a division of Macmillan Computer Publishing

Illustrations © 1994 Chris Kelly.

Library of Congress Catalog Number: 94-75809
ISBN: 1-56830-095-6

96   95   94   4   3   2

Interpretation of the printing code: the rightmost double-digit number is the year of the book's printing; the rightmost single-digit number is the number of the book's printing. For example, a printing code of 94-1 shows that the first printing of the book occurred in 1994.

The Hayden Books Team

Publisher *David Rogelberg*

Managing Editor *Karen Whitehouse*

Development Editor *Ruffin Prevost*

Production Editor *Brian Gill*

Interior Designer *Barbara Webster*

Cover Designer *Mirelez/Ross*

Production *Gary Adair, Dan Caparo, Brad Chinn, Kim Cofer, Lisa Daugherty, David Dean, Jennifer Eberhardt, Beth Rago, Bobbi Satterfield, Kris Simmons, Carol Stamile, Robert Wolf*

Composed in *Stone Serif, Stone San Serif, and MCPdigital*

To Our Readers

Dear Friend,

Thank you on behalf of everyone at Hayden Books for choosing *net.speak—the internet dictionary* to learn more about the Internet. It can be challenging to simply get on the "information highway," but this dictionary will help you navigate around technical terms, acronyms, slang, and jargon to maximize your time on the Internet. We have carefully crafted this book to provide a broad range of ideas and information.

What you think of this book is important to our ability to better serve you in the future. If you have any comments, no matter how great or small, we'd appreciate you taking the time to send us email, or a note by snail mail. Of course, we'd love to hear your book ideas.

Sincerely,

David Rogelberg
Publisher, Hayden Books and Adobe Press

Hayden Books
201 West 103rd Street
Indianapolis, IN 46290
(800) 428-5331 voice
(800) 448-3804 fax

email addresses:

America Online:	Hayden Bks
AppleLink:	hayden.books
CompuServe:	76350,3014
Internet:	hayden@hayden.com

Tom Fahey

Tom is the author of *The Joys of Jargon* and has been a technical writer and computer publishing consultant for Fortune 500 companies for the past 12 years. He has climbed Mt. Kilimanjaro to raise money for the end of hunger, and he enjoys fly fishing and lurking in fly fishing discussion groups on the Internet. If you have questions or comments about the book, Tom would be glad to hear from you. He can be reached at `faheyt@aol.com`.

Ruffin Prevost

Ruffin is a freelance writer and editor and sole proprietor of 4 A.M. Studios, a Los Angeles-based consulting firm. He has written and edited a number of books about the Macintosh, online services, and the Internet. He is a self-confessed Internet junkie, but wishes to point out that he really does have a life outside of cyberspace. He'll be glad to prove it to you if you'll just send him email at `ruffin@cerf.net`.

Acknowledgments

Tom would like to thank:

Jim Anders, author of *Live Wired: A Guide to Networking Macs* and master of computer networks—thanks for networking on a personal level and hooking me up with Hayden Books.

Mary Ann Hunsche and Dr. Sharon Marmon-Kaczorowski, colleagues who have become my friends—thanks for sharing your talents and energy when I needed them.

Debbie Goedken, of Lightfoot Graphics—thanks once more for helping me make a deadline.

Al Smith, computer wiz and neighbor—thanks for running those Internet errands for me.

Karen Whitehouse of Hayden Books—thanks for your trust and support over the long-distance phone lines.

Ruffin Prevost—thanks for editing and enhancing my book as though it were your own.

My incredible wife, Suzanne, and my brilliant sons, Colin and Chris—thanks for being in my life.

Ruffin would like to thank Gary Watson, Peter Vanderlinden, Terry Chan, Brad Heim, John Winston, Terry Smith, and Jonathan Monsarrat.

For Internet access and open-minded cooperation, Kent England at CERFnet.

Introduction

If you've ever wondered what's the difference between a bridger and a router (or, heaven forbid, what a brouter might be), then this book is for you. If listening to Internet authority figures babble about the Simple Network Management Protocol is your idea of a good time—then you may be better off putting this book down and spending your money on a subscription to *Switched Multimegabit Data Service Journal.*

For the rest of us, *net.speak* offers a place to turn for simple, clearly-stated explanations for the words, terms, slang, and catch phrases you hear the computer jocks spewing every time you hang around your company's dot matrix printers for more than three minutes. What's more, you'll also find in these pages plenty of tips on everything from what those bizarre symbols in email mean, to why you shouldn't post messages in ALL CAPS.

You'll find amusing stories and anecdotes that help explain the difference between Internet resources with names like CARL, EDGAR, and VERONICA. You'll learn the difference between asking Gopher to fetch a file and using Fetch to go for a file. You'll even read about people who enjoy tricking other folks into engaging in long, protracted fights where they have to type out their insults to each other.

How to Use This Book

Arranged in the convenient and time-tested format of alphabetical order, you'll find words like "access" and "binary" near the front of the book, and words like "virus" and "zone" at the back, with most others falling somewhere in between. Keep an eye out for the Tip icon. It marks words and terms that contain a particularly helpful bit of information that can save you time or money on the Net.

Naturally, there will be words you'll want to look up that you may not find listed here. If you've got a favorite word or phrase that didn't make it into this edition of *net.speak,* send it in. We'll do our best to include it in the next edition.

Contents

10Base2 An Ethernet wiring specification using "thin" coaxial cable. The notation translates as follows: "10" is its bandwidth—10Mbps; "base" stands for baseband (one channel); and "2" means it supports transmission over a segment of 200 meters. A 10Base2 system can wire together 30 devices. Known among LAN-snobs as "cheapernet" or "thinnet." *See also* coaxial cable.

10Base5 The original Ethernet wiring specification using "thick" coaxial cable (3/8"). The notation translates as follows: "10" is its bandwidth—10Mbps; "base" stands for baseband (one channel); and "5" means it supports transmission over a segment of 500 meters. A 10Base5 system can wire together 100 devices. 10Base5 has two layers of insulation and is popularly known as "thicknet." *See also* coaxial cable.

10BaseF An Ethernet wiring specification for fiber optic cable. The notation translates as follows: "10" is its bandwidth—10Mbps; "base" stands for baseband (one channel); and "F" means fiber. At the present, 10BaseF transmits at only 10Mbps, although the medium itself is broadband (many channels). The specification allows for future changes. *See also* coaxial cable.

10BaseT The latest Ethernet wiring specification using two pairs of unshielded twisted-pair 24 AWG (American Wire Gauge) wire. The notation translates as follows: "10" is its bandwidth—10Mbps; "base" stands for baseband (one channel); and "T" means twisted-pair. Sometimes called "UTP (Unshielded Twisted Pair) Ethernet." *See also* coaxial cable.

56K A type of telephone circuit that is sometimes called a "DDS" or an "ADN line." It is actually registered at 64K bps, but 8K bps are used for signaling.

64K A 64K bps circuit, also known as a "DSO line." When the entire bandwidth of 64K is used, it is called "Clear Channel."

666 bps The speed modems are said to run at when possessed by demonic forces preventing them from achieving their full data throughput rate.

802.x A series of standards established by the Institute of Electrical and Electronic Engineering (IEEE). The following table describes the specific standards.

Standard	Description
802.1	LAN bridges and network management.
802.2	Addressing and data link control (layers one and two of the OSI Reference Model). Also referred to as the Logical Link Control (LLC) sub-layer.
802.3	Ethernet LAN technology. This standard describes the Carrier Sense Multiple Access/Collision Detection (CSMA/CD) method of network access.
802.4	The use of the token passing on a bus network. This standard deals with LANs using the Manufacturing Automation Protocol (MAP).
802.5	The token ring network access method. This standard was developed based on IBM's Token Ring LAN.

3270 A series of IBM terminals that interact with IBM mainframes in a Virtual Machine (VM) environment.

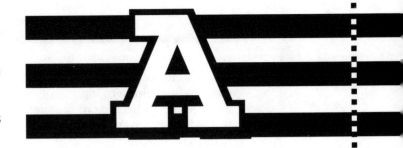

@   The "at" sign is used to separate the domain name and the user name in an Internet address. It is read and pronounced as "at" when describing an Internet address. For instance, the address `randy@eff.org` would be read as "randy at EFF dot org."

a21 Communications   A U.S. Internet provider in California. For information, send email to `info@rahul.net`.

AARNet   An Australian Internet provider. For information, send email to `aarnet@aarnet.edu.au`.

AARP   *See* **AppleTalk Address Resolution Protocol**.

AAUI   *See* **Apple Attachment Unit Interface**.

ABE   A DOS program that encodes a binary file so it can be sent by email. This method is a convenient way of sending and receiving files among people who have email access to the Internet, but lack file-transfer capabilities.

abstract syntax   A data structure specification that is generic and not limited to a particular computer or software.

Abstract Syntax Notation One (ASN.1)   An OSI protocol language that specifies abstract syntax. It also is used to encode SNMP packets.

Acceptable Use Policies (AUP)   A means of regulating the content of a message on the Internet, such as banning commercial use of the Internet on an educational or research network. The most significant AUP is the one published by NSFNET that specifically forbids "use for for-profit activities" and "extensive… personal business." AUP-free means the network, such as the Commercial Internet Exchange (CIX), does not restrict communications. For more information, see the sidebar "Make Money Fast" on the following page.

Make Money Fast

For most of its existence, the Internet has been free from commercial interference of any kind. But in the last few years, the Net has undergone radical changes, and commercial use of the Net has exploded. Despite the thousands of people and corporations doing business on the Internet, longtime "netizens" are often still surprised to see commercial traffic.

Partly because the Internet's acceptable use policies don't encourage it, and partly because it simply hasn't been done that much, widespread commercial advertising on the Internet has been a rarity—until recently. When one new Internet user innocently posted to several newsgroups a chain-letter style notice titled "Make Money Fast," he was swamped with hundreds of letters pointing out that his post was—at the least—bad netiquette, certainly annoying, and maybe even illegal. The mountains of flame-mail prompted a rare public apology posted in dozens of places around the net.

"I am sorry and feel deep remorse for the blatant abuse of Internet privileges," the user (who won't be identified, having suffered enough already) wrote. "I would like a second chance from you all to prove that I am not an ass. Please accept my apology, Internet, and understand the regret that I feel."

That user's posting wasn't the first—or the last—commercial posting to numerous newsgroups. For more on the creeping influence of capitalistic interests on the Net, see the sidebar "Spam-a-Go-Go" on page 170.

■■■■■■■■■■■

Access Control List (ACL)   A list of services provided by a site and the hosts authorized to use those services.

access   To make use of; to connect to; to log on to a computer. When Lt. Cmdr. Data on "Star Trek: The Next Generation" says he's "accessing," he means he's using his positronic brain to recall, analyze, or store information. When the rest of us use the word "access," it means we're interacting with a computer, or some part of a computer or network.

access method   The way in which a computer on a network determines when it can transmit data on a shared channel.

access privileges   *See* **privileges**.

access provider   *See* **service provider**.

account   A method of controlling access to a computer system by assigning unique login IDs (usernames) and passwords to individuals. Accounts are usually given a well-defined set of access privileges.

ACK   An acknowledgment from one computer to another that a block of data sent has been successfully received. The user does not see this message. If the block has not been successfully received, the computer returns a negative acknowledgment (NAK). *Contrast* NAK. *See also* checksum.

ACL   *See* **Access Control List**.

ACM   *See* **Association for Computing Machinery**.

active star   A network laid out in a star shape with all wiring leading to a concentrator or multiport repeater located at the center of the star. The star is said to be "active" because the concentrator retransmits the network signal from one branch of the star to the others. *Contrast* passive star.

AD   *See* **Administrative Domain**.

Add/Strip   A Macintosh utility that either inserts or deletes the carriage returns at the end of each line. This is useful for preparing text for email messages or for converting text files downloaded from the Internet. Add/Strip is a $25 shareware program by Jon Wind.

Address Mapping Table (AMT)   A table of physical addresses and their associated logical addresses. *See also* physical and logical.

Address Resolution Protocol (ARP)   A TCP/IP protocol that finds the IP address corresponding to a physical address. ARP is only available in systems that can send broadcast packets to all hosts on the network.

address   The name or number sequence that uniquely identifies each computer, printer, host, or other device on a network. There are also addresses identifying users. Internet users are mostly concerned with two addresses: computer addresses (so they can access different host computers to retrieve files), and personal addresses (so they can send email).

Computers on the Internet have two addresses. They have a domain name address, which is a text-type name, for example orion.oac.uci.edu.

They also have an Internet Protocol address (a numeric identifier sometimes called an "IP address," a "dot address," or simply "Internet address"), for example 132.25.44.1.

People who have an account on a computer directly connected to the Internet have a personal address that takes the form name@domain name—where name is the account name or username assigned to them, and domain name is the computer or system on which they are registered. For example pete@apple.com. *See also* mail address.

There are two categories of addresses: physical and logical. A physical address applies to a hardware device (or part of a device) that is by nature limited in quantity and location. A logical address applies to entities that are not limited in number or location. A single physical device can have multiple logical addresses.

address bus   The path within a computer through which information is passed about memory addresses, which are the locations where information will be read or written.

address commands   Connect extensions that provide enhanced functions for UUCP.

address mask   A code identifying the network and subnet portions of an IP address. Since it is mainly used to find out the subnet portion (the network portion is in the IP address), the address mask is sometimes referred to as the "subnet mask."

address resolution   The process of matching a physical address with a logical address.

Adidasnet   *See* **sneakernet**.

ADJ   The Boolean ADJACENT operator. When you place ADJ between two terms in a search request, the search is limited to text that has both terms next to

each other. For example, "george ADJ washington" finds all George Washingtons in the database.

Administrative Domain (AD)   The computers, routers, and networks managed by a single administrator.

ADSP   *See* **AppleTalk Data Stream Protocol**.

Advance Networks and Services (ANS)   A worldwide Internet provider in Michigan. For information, send email to maloff@nis.ans.net.

Advanced Interactive Executive (AIX)   IBM's version of UNIX.

Advanced Program-to-Program Communications (APPC)   Describes how peer-to-peer communications take place in an IBM SNA network between computers with the same processing capabilities. *See also* LU6.2 and Systems Network Architecture.

AEP   *See* **AppleTalk Echo Protocol**.

AFP   *See* **AppleTalk Filing Protocol**.

AFS   *See* **Andrew File system**.

agent   1) The component of a client/server system that prepares information and exchanges data for a client or server application.

2) A management program that is used by the Simple Network Management Protocol (SNMP) to collect information about network activity.

3) A buzzword used by marketing types (especially when describing "intelligent agents") to hype automated information search-and-retrieval methods. While some rudimentary "intelligent agents" do exist, the general consensus is that they're not yet ready for widespread use by the general public.

AI *See* **Artificial Intelligence**.

AIX *See* **Advanced Interactive Executive**.

alias A shorter form of a long name, such as an email address, a directory, or a command. With most email programs, you can set up aliases (sometimes called "nicknames") for individuals or groups. For example, rather than typing pete_smith@orion.oac.uci.edu in the address header, you can use an alias, "pete." If you need to reach a group of people, say the physics department, you simply could enter "physics" as an alias and your email program would automatically insert the email addresses of everyone in the physics department. Actually, all text-type addresses, long or short, are aliases of the IP address which is numerical only.

In DEC's VMS terminology, "logical name" is roughly equivalent to an alias.

To get an idea of the variety and creativity of people's aliases, just find out who's logged into a conference by typing the UNIX command "who." The system will spew out a list of monikers such as "Rapture, Kwalk, Shoyer, Rdjay, Lucyf, Big_j, Anitas, Wjo, Brianwideman, Jrnyfan, Cheryllynn Redduke, Game, Owellp, Smoker, Hawk7, Jbeyman, Jimrr4, Randbo, Billusmcret, Thunderfoot, Rock4, Chasb0058, Ultraviolet, Quercus, Lcmetz, Marcia901, Microscan, Ldigiorgi, Stevecrowley, Kevb, Ck17, Texasweet..."

Enough already!

ALL-IN-1 A Digital email and conference program that runs on VAX/VMS computers.

Alternative News Groups Hierarchy Usenet News Groups that were added to the original seven categories by popular demand. Following is a sampling of some of them:

Category	Topic
biz	business discussions
bionet	biological sciences
clari	commercial news services fed through ClariNet
bit	various BitNet newsgroups including some LISTSERV lists

TIP

America Online (AOL)   An online service with a direct Internet connection as opposed to CompuServe and Prodigy, which have email access only. Through the America Online (AOL) Internet Center, you can read from and post to newsgroups, subscribe to mailing lists, access Gopher, and search the World-Wide Web. Because of its easy-to-use graphical interface, America Online is the nation's fastest-growing online information service, currently boasting more than 800,000 subscribers. But AOL's growth-rate may stall out if folks can't get up the on-ramp to the information highway. America Online has licensed its interface software to Apple Computer for use in their eWorld online service. To contact an America Online user type user@aol.com.

American National Standards Institute (ANSI)   The predominant U.S. organization that develops voluntary standards for American industry. It helps to define network protocols and standards. ANSI standards such as ASCII is ANSI X3.4 are a familiar part of the computer landscape. The members of the American National Standards Institute meet with their international counterparts in the ISO body.

American Wire Gauge (AWG)   The standard for specifying the diameter of a wire. The larger the AWG number, the smaller the diameter. Since the number notation may appear to be counter-intuitive, think of the AWG as being the number of wires that can fit into a given space. Twenty-six strands of AWG26 wire can fit into the same area as 22 AWG22 strands.

amplitude   The spread between the minimum and maximum voltage of an electrical signal.

AMT *See* **Address Mapping Table**.

analog Said of a device that records or transmits continuous variations—as opposed to a digital device, that processes discontinuous pieces (chunks of numbers). Analog comes from the idea that there is an analogy between two physical things. For example, a person's voice is an analog of the strength of the audio signal being produced by a conventional telephone. A digital phone, on the other hand, takes the person's voice and converts it into a series of numbers. A phonograph record (remember them?) is analog: its grooves correspond to the sounds being produced, the louder the sound, the deeper the groove. Compact disks are digital. Watches with hands and mercury-tube thermometers are analog, which is another way of saying "old-fashioned." *See also* digital and modem.

AND The Boolean AND operator. When you place AND between two terms in a search request, a database service such as Veronica will limit searches to text that satisfies both criteria. For example, searching for "dog AND cat" will produce a list of only those items that have both "dog" and "cat" in them, but not files that have only "dog" or only "cat" in them.

Andrew File system (AFS) A suite of protocols that enables you to use files on other network computers as though they were local.

anonymous FTP A service that enables you to connect to a remote computer by logging on as an anonymous user and thereby sidestepping local security. Even though it sounds shady, this is a legitimate and widely accepted way of accessing many gigabytes of public files stored on thousands of computers across the Internet. Administrators have set up host computers so that you can access certain portions of their contents by logging in under the name "anonymous." Usually, as a courtesy, you enter your full user name with domain name as a password so a record of usage can be kept. Some locations only ask that you type "guest" as the password. Regardless, most FTP sites can keep track of who logs in and out regardless of who does or doesn't enter his or her user name.

How FTP Works

FTP enables you to transfer files from your computer to a host, from a host to your computer, or between hosts. It is mainly used in the second manner—namely, to copy files from a remote host to the one you are logged on to (the local host). The standard way to start the program is to type "ftp" followed by the host name. For example:

```
% ftp nic.merit.edu
```

If you simply type "ftp," you will get the ftp prompt. At this point you can use the "open" command to access a remote host. When you are connected, you will be prompted for a name, which is where you enter "anonymous." Here is an example:

```
ftp>open nic.merit.edu

Connected to nic.merit.edu.

220 nic.merit.edu FTP server (SunOS 4.1) ready.

Name (nic.merit.edu:smith): anonymous

331 Guest login ok, send ident as password.

Password: smith@orion.oac.uci.edu

230 Guest login ok, access restrictions apply.
```

Now that you are connected to the host, you can view the directory by typing dir. (The directory contents are only partially shown below.)

```
ftp> dir

200 PORT command successful.

150 ASCII data connection for /bin/ls
(158.130.2.3,1741) (0 bytes).

total 58

-rw-r—r— 1 nic    merit    21219 Feb 11 02:30 INDEX

-rw-r—r— 1 nic    merit    16326 Oct 22 23:18 READ.ME
```

To download the READ.ME file, enter the get command:

```
ftp> get READ.ME

local: READ.ME remote: READ.ME
```

```
200 PORT command successful.

150 ASCII data connection for READ.ME
(158.130.2.3,1742) (16326 bytes).

226 ASCII Transfer complete.

16677 bytes received in 0.59 seconds (27.60 Kbytes/s)
```

To conclude the session, enter the "bye" command.

If this seems like a bit much to go through to download a READ.ME file, you might consider using a graphical FTP program such as Fetch for the Macintosh which enables you to set up shortcuts and automatically log on to FTP servers and then transfer files by selecting buttons.

■ ■ ■ ■ ■ ■ ■ ■ ■ ■

anonymous FTP host An Internet computer that provides access to public files.

ANS *See* **Advanced Networks and Services**.

ANSI *See* **American National Standards Institute**.

AOL *See* **America Online**.

API *See* **Application Program Interface**.

APPC *See* **Advanced Program-to-Program Communications**. *See also* attachment.

append To attach one file to another for transmission. Many email systems have an attachment feature that enables you to mail a file along with your message. You can send ASCII text files or binary files (such as spreadsheets or word processing documents) that contain special formatting. The receiver of the message with the appended file will be asked by the email system where to store the file. Once the file is stored on the recipient's computer, it can be opened with the appropriate software. When you append a file, you should make sure that the recipient's email system can handle the file. Some systems enable the transfer of audio and graphic files as well. *See also* Multipurpose Internet Mail Extensions.

Apple Attachment Unit Interface (AAUI) Apple's interface to Ethernet that consists of a connector, an external transceiver, and cabling.

AppleDouble An Apple file format that enables you to store Macintosh files on another computing system and share those files with non-Macintosh users. AppleDouble separates the data fork and the resource fork and places them into different files. *Contrast* AppleSingle.

appendixware A particularly useless category of software (usually shareware) that performs a task so specific or trivial as to be virtually meaningless to the general population at large. One such program, Temperament, deletes annoying Microsoft Word temporary files that linger on the hard drives of unsuspecting users. The Net is full of appendixware.

. . . . **TIP** . . . .

AppleLink Apple Computer's graphical online information service. Apple employees, third-party developers, and the media use AppleLink to send email and get product updates. To contact someone on AppleLink, use this format:
user@applelink.apple.com.

AppleLink packages AppleLink's archive and compression format that can be decompressed by StuffIt Expander.

AppleShare Apple's file server software that uses the AFP protocol.

AppleShare file server A Macintosh computer that runs the AppleTalk Filing Protocol (AFP).

AppleSingle An Apple file format that places both the data fork and the resource fork of Macintosh files into a single file. *Contrast* AppleDouble.

AppleTalk Apple's local area networking software. It enables Apple computers to communicate and share resources with each other. This protocol is independent of the network layer on which it is run. It currently is implemented as LocalTalk and EtherTalk.

AppleTalk/DECnet Transport Gateway A gateway that is part of AppleTalk for VMS that enables Macintosh computers to access DECnet-based applications, such as email and DECwindows.

AppleTalk Address Resolution Protocol (AARP) Apple's protocol for storing logical AppleTalk node addresses and corresponding physical hardware addresses.

AppleTalk address A three-part number that uniquely identifies a software process on an AppleTalk network.

AppleTalk Data Stream Protocol (ADSP) A session layer protocol. ADSP provides a reliable stream of data between two sockets in an AppleTalk network.

AppleTalk Echo Protocol (AEP) An AppleTalk Transport layer protocol. AEP enables a node to determine if a signal reaches another node and the round-trip delivery time. It accomplishes this by sending a packet to the other node and receiving an echoed response.

AppleTalk Filing Protocol

(AFP) An AppleTalk Presentation layer protocol. AFP defines shared file access and is the basis for AppleShare.

AppleTalk for VMS
An AppleTalk network protocol suite that runs on VMS, Digital's operating system for VAX computers. By setting up VAX computers as AppleTalk nodes, AppleTalk for VMS enables services such as the VAXshare file server to be connected as AppleTalk sockets.

AppleTalk Remote Access

(ARA) Apple software that enables one Macintosh to access another "remote" Macintosh and use both local or network resources such as servers and printers on another "remote" computer. The local Macintosh connects to the remote computer via a modem and software that is based on either AppleShare and/or Personal File Sharing.

AppleTalk Session Protocol

(ASP) An AppleTalk Session layer protocol that defines the interactions of two devices once they are in communication and have established a session. ASP specifies the process of opening and closing of a session, sending commands and replies between devices, and ensuring that the connection continues throughout the session

AppleTalk Transaction Protocol

(ATP) An AppleTalk Transport layer protocol that ensures that packets arrive at their intended destination. ATP deals with re-quests and responses that have become lost or delayed in the transmission process.

AppleTalk-LAT connection

tool A tool in Apple's Communications Toolbox that enables the AppleTalk-LAT Gateway to access LAT terminal services over LocalTalk or AppleTalk Remote Access sessions.

AppleTalk-LAT Gateway
A part of DEC's PATHWORKS for Macintosh that runs on a Macintosh and is used to translate AppleTalk protocols into LAT protocols.

Application Layer
Layer seven (the top) of the OSI Reference Model defines the protocols for the interaction between applications and communication services, effecting file transfers, email, and terminal functions.

Application Programming Interface

(API) Communications routines for the transfer of data and commands between a program and other software or hardware such as a network interface card. *See also* Socket Programming Interface.

application
A software program that you directly interact with when using a computer. For example, word processors, databases, and spreadsheets are all applications.

ARA
See **AppleTalk Remote Access**.

■■■

ARC   A file extension abbreviation used by DOS computers.

■ ■ ■ ■ ■ ■ ■ ■ **TIP** ■ ■ ■ ■ ■ ■ ■ ■

Archie   A database service that indexes and catalogs files on Internet hosts. With more than two billion files stored on anonymous FTP computers around the Internet, locating a specific file seems almost hopeless. Archie enables you to find the needle in the electronic haystack. Developed by McGill School of Computer Science, Archie resides on "Archie servers." Some are shown in the following table.

■ ■

Archie Servers

Address	*Description*
archie.rutgers.edu	Rutgers University
archie.sura.net	SURAnet server
archie.unl.edu	University of Nebraska in Lincoln
archie.ans.net	ANS server
archie.au	Australian server
archie.funet.fi	European server in Finland
archie.doc.ic.ac.uk	UK/England server
archie.cs.huji.ac.il 1	Israeli server
archie.wide.ad.jp	Japanese server
archie.ncu.edu.tw	Taiwanese server

You can access Archie in three ways: 1) email, 2) telneting to an archie server, and 3) through archie client software.

In all three methods, you are sending a request to an Archie server and it returns the name of files matching your criteria and the name of the site where it is stored.

Archie-by-Telnet Commands

about	Information about Archie.
bugs	Bugs and undesirable features.
bye, exit, quit	Quits Archie.

continued

14

continues

help	Online help.
list	Lists the sites in the Archie database.
mail	Mails output.
nopager or unset pager	Cancels page-at-a-time display.
pager or set pager	Sets page-at-a-time display.
prog	Searches the database for a file.
set	Sets a variable.
show	Shows variable settings.
site	Lists the files at an archive site.
term or set term	Specifies terminal type.
unset	Unsets a variable.
whatis	Searches for a keyword in the software description database.

See also Whatis and Software Description Database.

Archie for Nextstep   Nextstep Archie client software. Available by anonymous FTP at `sonata.cc.purdue.edu`.

Archie for the Macintosh
Macintosh Archie client software. Available by anonymous FTP at `sumex-aim.stanford.edu`.

archive   (Noun) 1) The place on an internet host where files are stored. 2) A file that contains a number of compressed files.

(Verb) To compress a number of files into one file for storage and transmittal. *See also* compress and extract.

archive site   A computer dedicated to the storage of files, usually organized by subject, that can be accessed through anonymous FTP or email. Also known as a file site or FTP site. Most files stored at archive sites are compressed and need to be extracted to be used.

ARCnet   Attached Resource Computer NETwork. An LAN standard developed by Datapoint Corporation, ARCnet uses a media-access control method that is similar to token-passing. Each network interface card is assigned a unique number at installation. A master card maintains a table of all the card numbers on the LAN and polls them before giving one permission to transmit. ARCnet uses a star topology with both active and passive hubs and can extend the cabling farther than Ethernet or Token Ring. It can use either coaxial or twisted-pair cabling and has a signaling speed of 2.5 Mbps.

ARCnet Plus   A 1992 release of ARCnet that has 20 Mbps signaling.

ARP   *See* **Address Resolution Protocol**.

arp   Command used to view or update the Address Resolution Protocol table.

ARPA   Advanced Research Projects Agency. This agency of the U.S. Department of Defense, in partnership with universities and other research communities, built ARPANET, the precursor to the Internet. Its general mission is to develop new technology for military use. ARPA provided funding for the development of the Berkeley version of UNIX and TCP/IP. ARPA had undergone a bureaucratic identity crises over the years— it was originally ARPA, then changed its name to DARPA ("D" for Defense), and finally went back to ARPA in 1993.

ARPANET   Advanced Research Projects Agency Network. The first packet-switching network and the prototype of Internet was launched in an experimental mode in 1969. ARPANET consisted of individual packet-switching computers interconnected by leased lines. ARPANET grew in size to include 300 computers by 1983, split into two networks in 1984 (the other

one being MILNET), and was disbanded in 1990.

article   A single news item posted to a Usenet newsgroup. *See also* posting.

Artificial Intelligence (AI)   One of the goals of computer scientists is to create a machine that thinks and learns like human beings. The phrase "artificial intelligence" was coined by John McCarthy at M.I.T. in 1956.

Alan Turing came up with a way to test whether a computer is actually thinking. The test involves having a computer carry on a conversation with a person in such a natural way that the person does not know he or she is actually talking to a computer. So far, no computer comes close to passing the test, and from looking at some of the contributions to online "chats," it seems as though some humans wouldn't pass the test either.

AS   *See* **Autonomous System**.

ASCII   American Standard Code for Information Interchange. A data transmission standard for assigning seven-bit codes to 128 different elements including the 26 letters of the alphabet in upper and lower case, the basic number set (0-9), and punctuation marks. In addition, there are control characters, including printer-type commands such as line feed and carriage return, and telecommunication-type commands such as ACK, NAK, XON, and XOFF. ASCII is the lowest common denominator among different computer applications. It is non-proprietary and virtually all programs and platforms can read and transmit ASCII files. While ASCII cannot handle advanced attributes such as color and graphics, it's the standard for text-only file transfers across the Internet. Pronounced "ASK-key." *Contrast* EBCDIC and unicode.

AskERIC   A resource of the Educational Resources Information Center (ERIC) that enables you to obtain information about educational services available through the Internet. To contact them, send email to: askeric@ricir.syr.edu

ASN.1   *See* **Abstract Syntax Notation One**.

ASP   *See* **AppleTalk Session Protocol**.

assigned numbers   Values assigned by the Internet Assigned Numbers Authority (IANA) for links, sockets, ports, and protocols used in network protocol implementations.

Association for Computing Machinery (ACM)   Established in 1947, this organization promotes computer research and development.

Asynchronous Transfer Mode (ATM)   A standard for a cell-switching network that defines the technology for handling heavy data loads and transmission speeds of 1.544 megabits per second to 1.2 gigabits per second. This method calls for the dynamic

allocation of bandwidth. ATM is also known as "fast packet."

asynchronous   A transmission method that does not require sender and receiver to be synchronized. Unlike synchronous transmission, data is not sent at a precise time. Each character must be preceded by a "start" bit and followed by a "stop" bit. Familiarly referred to as "async." Compare and contrast with synchronous and bisynchronous.

AT commands   Modem "attention" commands. The string "AT" must precede all modem commands, except for +++ and A/. The following table shows the most common AT commands, with "AT" preceding the actual command where necessary. *See also* initialization string.

Athene   An online fiction magazine. You can reach it via anonymous FTP at quartz.rutgers.edu.

ATM   *See* **Asynchronous Transfer Mode**. (It also stands for the ubiquitous Automated Teller Machine, Adobe Type Manager, and a dozen other things. It just happens to be a popular letter combination.)

atob   ASCII to binary. A UNIX program that translates ASCII files into binary files for sending by email. Pronounced "a to b." *Contrast* btoa.

Modem AT commands

Command	Description
+++	Escape code.
A/	Repeat last AT command.
AT	Attention code. Precedes all commands except "+++" and "A/".
AT&Fn	Restore modem to factory configuration.
AT&Ln	Toggle between leased line and dial-up line operation.
AT&Tn	Select test mode option.
AT&V	View stored parameters.
AT&Zn=Z	Store telephone numbers.
ATA	Answer incoming call.
ATDPn or ATDTn	Dial command – P for pulse (no Touch-Tone) and T for Tone, n stands for the phone number. If you want to turn-off call waiting, type #70 or 1170 before the phone number.
ATEn	Command echo - toggles the "echoing" of commands to the screen. E0 is echo OFF and E1 echo ON.
ATHn	Hook control.
ATIn	Identification.
ATLn	Speaker volume.
ATOn	Return to online state.
ATP	Set pulse dialing as the default.
ATT	Set tone dialing as default.
ATZn	Reset.

ATP *See* **AppleTalk Transaction Protocol**.

Attachment Unit Interface (AUI) A multipin-connector on an Ethernet piece of equipment that interfaces to a transceiver.

attachment A file that is sent along with an email message. The file can be text or binary, such as a database, an application program, or a formatted word-processing document.

attenuation The weakening of an electrical signal during transmission.

AUI   *See* **Attachment Unit Interface**.

AUP   *See* **Acceptable Use Policies**.

authentication   A method for validating the identity of the sender of a message.

auto select   A newsreader feature that enables you to specify criteria so that certain articles are automatically displayed. *Contrast* kill.

Autonomous System (AS)   A set of routers administered by a single authority that uses a common Interior Gateway Protocol for routing packets.

AWG   *See* **American Wire Gauge**.

B   Standard abbreviation for one byte. Usually eight bits. *See also* octet.

b   Standard abbreviation for one bit. There are eight bits in one byte.

backbone or backbone network   A network connecting other networks. Backbone networks, such as NSFNET, are the eight-lane superhighways of the Internet. Generally, the term refers to a high-performance network of thick Ethernet wire or fiber-optic cable that enables data transmission among lower-performance networks. The networks that connect to backbones are referred to as stub and transit networks. Sometimes, backbone refers to the system of wires, cross connects, and cables in a specific building.

backspace   On the top row of IBM keyboards, backspace is the key with the left arrow. On Macintosh computers, the backspace function is served by the left arrow key, which moves the cursor to the left one space. The large key labeled "delete" is a destructive backspace: it deletes the character to the left of the cursor.

balanced line   A transmission medium in which the wires it contains are electrically equal, such as twisted-pair wire. *See also* unbalanced line.

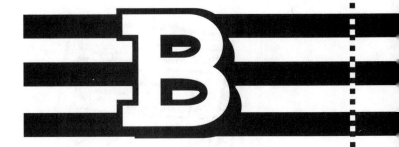

balun   From balanced/unbalanced. A device that connects a balanced line to an unbalanced line. In a balanced line (such as a twisted-pair wire), the wires are electrically equal. In an unbalanced line (such as a coaxial cable), the central conductor is not electrically equal to the shield.

bandwidth   The amount of data that can travel through a circuit expressed in bits per second. (Note that this measures capacity, not speed.) The greater the bandwidth, the greater the amount of data the line can handle. Technically, bandwidth is the width of a transmission line measured in Hertz. *See also* wasted bandwidth.

bang   An exclamation point!

bang path   An email address that employs an exclamation point (!) to separate the names of different computers that make up the path through which the mail is to be routed. An UUCP network form.

banner A header or message sent by a system administrator that displays automatically when you invoke a command. For example, when selecting "email" on Delphi, a statement about addressing messages appears. It's very helpful the first time you use email, but once you learn the basics, the banner is a nuisance. In this case, the Delphi administrator thoughtfully will tell you how to avoid the banner in the future.

Deep Purple

It's tough to explain exactly why or how the Internet's Barney fixation evolved, but among many newsgroup regulars, there's an interest in Barney the Dinosaur that borders on an obsessive-compulsive disorder.

Parents forced to watch the Purple One's "Barney & Friends" kids' show on PBS have no doubt experienced some of the concern many netizens feel over Barney's widespread control of their children's attention.

To experience outright hatred and loathing of Barney first-hand, check out any of several Barney-related newsgroups (start with `alt.Barney.die.die.die`). A deeper exploration into the purple passions over Barney will reveal a netwide holy war between various sects and churches devoted to the destruction of Barney and all that he stands for and, conversely, the exaltation of Barney to god-like status.

TIP

BARRNET A San Franciso, CA area and Far East Internet provider. For information, send email to gd.why@forsythe.standford.edu.

baseband A type of transmission that takes the entire bandwith, or capacity, of the cabling to send a signal. LAN systems (for example, LocalTalk, Ethernet, and Token Ring) are typically baseband: one channel of data is transmitted at a time. *Contrast* broadband.

Basic Encoding Rules (BER)   A standard data unit encoding technique defined in ASN.1. *See also* Abstract Syntax Notation One.

basic rate interface (BRI)   An Integrated Services Digital Network (ISDN) service that enables LANs to link via two data channels that each operate at 64 kilobits per second.

batch   A method of organizing several files into a single group for transmitting or printing. This increases the efficiency of the data transmission. Referred to as batch mode.

baud   The speed of a modem. A measure of the number of times per second a communications channel changes the carrier signal it sends on the phone line. A 9600-baud modem changes the signal 9600 times a second. Do not confuse baud with bits per second (bps), or the techie-pedants will jump all over you at rate of 9600 times a second.

BBS   *See* **Bulletin Board System**.

bcc   *See* **blind carbon copy**.

BCnet   A British Columbia Internet provider. For information, send email to BCnet@ubc.ca.

BCNU   Be seein' you. A common shorthand abbreviation seen in chat sessions and email messages.

BEM   Bug-Eyed Monster. A common shorthand abbreviation seen in chat sessions and email messages.

BER   *See* **Basic Encoding Rules**.

Berkeley Internet Name Domain (BIND)   A UNIX version of the Domain Name System developed and distributed by the University of California at Berkeley. BIND runs on many Internet hosts.

Berkeley Software Distribution (BSD)   A version of the UNIX operating system and its utilities developed and distributed by the University of California at Berkeley. The term "4.3 BSD" shows the version number of the distribution. BSD is common throughout the Internet.

BGP   *See* **Border Gateway Protocol**.

big-endian   A format for storing data in which the most significant byte is first. You may remember the Big-Endians in Jonathan Swift's *Gulliver's Travels*, who fought a 30-year war against the Little-Endians over the matter of which end of an egg should be broken first.

"It is computed, that eleven thousand persons have, at several times, suffered death, rather than submit to break their eggs at the smaller end."

Luckily the wars over where to place a string of bits have been purely verbal. *See also* little-endian.

Binary Synchronous Control (Bisync)   An IBM protocol at the data-link level of communications for devices operating in synchronous environments. Bisync defines operations such as the format of data frames that are sent through modems.

B

binary Made up of two parts. Computers use a binary number system, a sequence of ones and zeroes that tell the computer's switches to turn off ("0") and on ("1"). Fans (or victims) of New Math know this as base two.

binary file A non-ASCII file, such as a database or executable program, that contains data that is not text and therefore cannot be printed. An ASCII file is a 7-bit format. Applications, such as word processing programs, produce files that have 8-bit data. A binary file can only be sent by email by encoding it as a text file with a program such as unencode or BinHex. You can download a binary file with the FTP binary command. In speech, usually shortened to a single word as in "Send it binary."

BIND *See* **Berkeley Internet Name Domain**.

TIP

BinHex A Macintosh program that converts binary files to ASCII so that it can be sent by email. BinHex also can segment files if needed. A BinHex-converted file has the extension HQX.

BIOSIS/FS A database of biomedical and biological research that you can access through the Online Computer Learning Center (OCLC).

Birds Of a Feather (BOF) An ad hoc discussion group that flocks together for the purpose of examining a particular issue.

bis French for "repeat" or "ditto." Used in the V.xx series of modem standards. For example, V.42bis means the new standard is the same as V.42 with some additions.

Bisync *See* **Binary Synchronous Control**.

bisynchronous The transmission of information in two directions at a time. Telephone conversations are bisynchronous. Sender and receiver must be online at the same time. A bisynchronous line can have data moving from and to a terminal simultaneously. *See also* synchronous.

bit Short for binary digit. A computer only uses two digits: "0" (which turns an electrical circuit "off") and "1" (which turns an electrical signal "on"). A bit is a the smallest unit of information handled by a computer. There are eight bits in a single byte. *See also* byte, kilobyte, and megabyte.

BITNET Because It's Time Network. A network used by the academic and research community for email, mailing lists, and file transfers. It is distinct from the Internet but connected in some ways. It is mostly a collection of IBM and DEC mainframe computers. If you are on the Internet, you can't use telnet or FTP to access BITNET, but you can exchange email messages through special gateways. For example, with email you can access LISTSERV—a mailing list service of gigantic proportion that is maintained in BITNET. BITNET is part of the Corporation for Research and Networking (CREN). Its counterparts are NETNORTH in Canada and EARN in Europe.

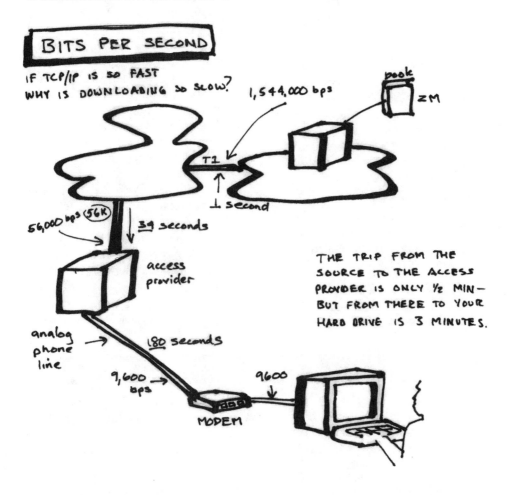

BITS PER SECOND

IF TCP/IP IS SO FAST WHY IS DOWNLOADING SO SLOW?

1,544,000 bps

book

2M

T1

1 second

56,000 bps (56K)

34 seconds

access provider

THE TRIP FROM THE SOURCE TO THE ACCESS PROVIDER IS ONLY ½ MIN — BUT FROM THERE TO YOUR HARD DRIVE IS 3 MINUTES.

analog phone line

180 seconds

9,600 bps

9600

MODEM

bits per second (bps) The number of bits that can be sent through a communication medium per second. For instance,10Kbps means 10,000 per second (the K stands for kilo—1000), while 5Mbps means five million bits per second (the M stands for mega—one million).

BIX *See* **BYTE Information Exchange**.

TIP

blind carbon copy (bcc)   When you use bcc, recipients of copies of your message do not know who else has also received a copy. *See also* cc. But beware, because the bcc feature is not completely compatible across-the-board throughout all corners of the Internet and the services with email gateways. Your blind carbon copy recipients may be clearly listed in the header or body of a message as carbon copy recipients or standard "co-recipients."

board   Common term for printer circuit boards, breadboards, and motherboards.

body   The part of the mail packet that contains the message you are sending to someone else. *See also* header.

BOF   *See* **Birds of a Feather**.

TIP

bookmark   A method of creating your own personal Gopher menu, thus bypassing the menu-upon-menu trek to your favorite Gopher hole. A menu-driven system is handy except when you have to tap out the same keystrokes over and over again to reach your destination. To add a bookmark, type "a" next to the menu entry you want. Later, you can view your bookmarks in menu arrangement by typing "v." Users with graphical Gopher-client software (such as TurboGopher on the Macintosh) can create bookmarks and post them on the Internet where others can download them and use them with their own Gopher programs.

Something for Everyone

Part of the beauty of the Net is how it directly reflects the diversity of its inhabitants. If you think you're the only person on the planet with a particular passion, interest, or avocation, think again. The smart money says you'll find a soulmate on the Internet. Just ask Nathan Torkington.

If your hero is Earl Scruggs and your idea of a good fight involves dueling banjos, then you should definitely check out Nathan Torkington's original and transcribed five-string banjo tablature archive.

It's there that you'll find tablatures for works from Mozart's "Turkish March" (from Piano Sonata #11 in A), Charlie Parker's "Barbados," and even original works by Torkington. Banjo fans can contact Torkington directly via email at nathan.torkington@vuw.ac.nz.

Boolean search   A method of finding information in a database or an online service using Boolean operators (for example, AND, OR, NOT). Used in Veronica. Named after George Boole.

BOOTP   *See* **Bootstrap Protocol**.

Bootstrap Protocol (BOOTP)   A protocol that is used for booting diskless nodes. *See also* Reverse Address Resolution Protocol.

Border Gateway Protocol (BGP)   An exterior gateway protocol that is defined in RFCs 1267 and 1268. BGP is a refinement of the Exterior Gateway Protocol (EGP) used by the NSFNET backbone network.

bounce   What happens to email messages with incorrect addresses, and checks with insufficient funds. When you bounce an email, your message is returned to you by the system's postmaster with a subject of "undeliverable mail." If you decipher the gobbledygook (perhaps by using this book), you can sometimes sort out what went wrong and try again. Not as embarrassing as bouncing a check, but sometimes just as frustrating.

Bourne shell   *See* **shell**.

bps   *See* **bits per second**.

BRI   *See* **basic rate interface**.

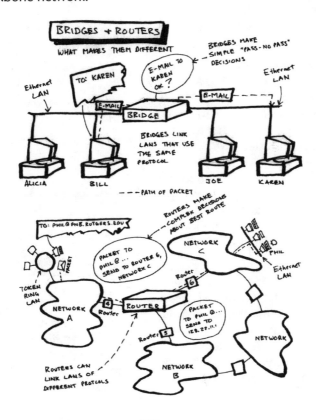

bridge A device connecting two or more network components that use the same protocols. A typical application for a bridge is to link two different workgroup LANs. The bridge examines the address of a transmission and determines whether it should be passed along to the next LAN or stay within the originating LAN. Bridges operate on the Data Link Layer. *See also* router.

brief A mode of displaying abbreviated commands and messages at the system prompt in an interactive session. For example, in brief mode, if you enter your workspace, the system prompt is "WS>" rather than "WORKSPACE>," which is what appears in verbose mode. You can toggle between brief and verbose on many systems.

broadband A type of transmission medium that carries multiple signals at a time. For example, a broadband coaxial cable can handle many cable TV channels at the same time. It deals with multiple signals by dividing the total capacity of the medium into separate, independent bandwidth channels, where each channel operates within a specific range of frequencies. *See also* baseband.

broadcast A transmission sent out to all network hosts. This is usually done when an administrator needs to inform users that the network is about to be shut down. A broadcast is a much more efficient way of reaching everyone on a network than passing the news to users one-at-a-time.

broadcast storm Bad weather on the network that arises when an erroneous packet is broadcast to the network, causing many hosts to respond all at once. Usually, the other hosts respond with their own erroneous packets. The result is a self-generating whirlwind of useless transmissions.

brouter A device that combines the functions a router and a bridge. It filters the traffic of transmissions, routing some types (based on data link layer information) and bridging others (based on network layer information). *See also* bridge and router.

BSD *See* **Berkeley Software Distribution**.

btoa A UNIX program that translates binary files into ASCII files for sending by email. Pronounced "b to a." *Contrast* atob.

BTW By the way. A common shorthand abbreviation seen in chat sessions and email messages.

buffer A part of a device's RAM that holds data until it can be processed. For instance, your communications software might temporarily store the contents of a display screen so that you can

scroll back to read it later. Some emulation packages have the capability of storing a specified amount of data or writing it to disk at your request. Some printers also have a buffer so that when a computer sends a multi-page document, the printer can "hold" the other pages in its buffer while it is printing one page. Having a buffer reduces interruptions in data flow between devices. *See also* handshaking.

Bulletin Board System (BBS)

A computer system you, and thousands of others, can use to send messages, exchange software, and keep up with the latest technical gossip. Hobbyists, academics, and bureaucrats flock to BBSs like birds to feeders. Once upon a time, your average BBS was purely local, but now it is likely to provide mail, telnet, FTP, and other Internet services. Many BBSs are administered by government, educational, and research organizations. There are now an estimated 10,000 BBSs in use throughout America. CompuServe, America Online, and Prodigy operate as BBSs on a large scale. Many BBSs offer a connection to the Internet and their participants can exchange mail with Internet users.

BBSs offer many services, including structured discussion groups. Some, but not all, BBSs are free. To set up a BBS, you need special software and a dedicated person to serve as system operator.

Bulletin Board System Operator (Sysop)

An individual who attends to the tasks of maintaining a BBS. A Sysop's duties include updating files, scanning for viruses, answering user queries, troubleshooting technical problems, and a host of other tasks that range from torture to ecstacy, depending on the sysop you talk to and when you talk to him or her (although it's usually a "him").

bus   1) A common network segment to which devices are connected. *See also* backbone network.

2) A group of wires that enable signals to be shared between devices on several circuit cards. Included in the bus are the data bus, control bus, and address bus. Also called a channel.

bus topology   A type of network in which devices are connected to a single cable. Also called a daisy chain. A bus topology is linear—meaning it has no loops or branches. This is the simplest and cheapest type of network; however, it is limited in scope. An Ethernet bus can support about 40 nodes.

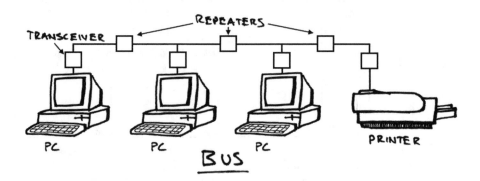

BUS TOPOLOGY

REPEATERS

TRANSCEIVER

PC

PC

PC

BUS

PRINTER

TIP

buzz words   Words that occur so frequently in documents they are meaningless in a search. WAIS database administrators maintain a list to filter out buzz that would tie up the service in endless retrievals. There are more than 700 words such as "able," "action," and "address" on the no-no list. *See also* stop words.

TIP

BYTE Information Exchange (BIX)   An online commercial information service that was spawned by *BYTE* magazine. You can reach BIX from an Internet site by telneting to x25.bix.com and entering "BIX" when the system prompts for a username.

byte   Generally used to mean a group of eight bits that are used to designate characters. Why 8? Because eight bits can be arranged in 256 unique ways, to form a standard set of alphanumeric and control characters, as well as special symbols and punctuation. Some systems, however, have what are called 7-bit bytes—the 7 bits of the ASCII code and a stop or start bit. To solve the confusion, an 8-bit byte is sometimes referred to as an octet. *See also* octet.

C A programming language that is widely used on UNIX systems.

C shell *See* **shell**.

Call For Votes (CFV) Part of the process for proposing and setting up a new newsgroup. After a discussion, you send out a "call for votes" and poll the participants to see if there is enough support to warrant setting up a new group.

Campus-Wide Information Server (CWIS) A system that provides a college or university community with online information about class schedules and special events, as well as providing directory information, calendars, bulletin boards, and databases. Higher education groups work with each other to solve problems and share CWIS resources.

capture Sending the contents of a computer's RAM buffer to a printer or to a disk. While online, it's often helpful to capture the text you encounter and store it on disk or print it out for later reference, especially if you pay for connect time.

card A printed circuit. Only older folks need to be told that "card" no longer refers to the punched card that said "Do Not Bend, Fold, Spindle Or Mutilate." The words "card" and "board" are often used synonymously, particularly when referring to a component installed in a PC, such as a network or graphics card/board.

CARL *See* **Colorado Alliance of Research Libraries**.

carpetnetter One with little experience in actually using the Net but great ambitions in exploiting it for commercial gain. Many wild-eyed corporate types see large dollar signs blinking on the modem displays of Net users across the country and are anxious to enslave net-savvy (but business-ignorant) technical types into fulfilling capitalistic dreams of cashing in on the Net's popularity. If carpetnetters succeed in their ultimate goal, the end result will be the total exploitation of the Net as a means to force-sell junk that folks don't need and, in fact, stuff they only want becuase they've been netnotized into thinking they must have it. *See also* netcropper.

carriage return   A command or control character that makes the cursor or printer head move to the beginning of the next line. The carriage return is a control character (ASCII 13) and is not printable. On a personal computer, you press the Return or Enter key to make a carriage return. In word processing programs, a carriage return is the same as an end-of-paragraph mark.

The term itself is a quaint holdover—obviously there are no carriages on personal computers. People who have used manual typewriters (probably the same folks who remember record players) are familiar with a "real" carriage return—it was a metal handle that you pushed when you reached the end of a line. This made the paper ratchet up a notch and the roller slide over so you could type the next line. It gave writers a feeling of satisfaction. But enough nostalgia. Technically, in the world of computers, a carriage return only returns the cursor to the beginning of the same line you are on. To advance a line, you need a carriage return/linefeed which is a distinct command. Different types of computers handle this differently. *See also* linefeed.

Carrier Sense Multiple Access (CSMA)   A method used by networks such as Ethernet and AppleTalk to enable multiple devices to access a single channel efficiently. "Carrier Sense" means that each device listens to the traffic on the network to determine if signals are passing or are about to pass—like a cowboy in an old Western putting his ear to a railroad track to hear the vibrations of a oncoming train. If the channel (or track) is clear, the device makes it known that it is going to transmit. Two enhancements are Collision Avoidance (CA) and Collision Detection (CD).

With Collision Avoidance, devices are programmed to "back off" if contention (simultaneous transmissions) occurs. Both devices will wait an instant before retransmitting to avoid butting heads again. The waiting time interval is random so there is little chance of both devices resuming transmissions at the same instant. An AppleTalk network system with LocalTalk cables uses CSMA/CA.

With Collision Detection, devices are programmed to listen while transmitting. They will know when a collision has occurred because the signals they hear are different than the ones they transmitted and they did not receive an acknowledgment from the receiving device. As in Collision Avoidance, devices that have detected a collision will wait a random time interval before retransmitting. Ethernet networks use CSMA/CD.

carrier   A continuous frequency produced by modems over the telephone lines during transmission. The carrier serves as a reference signal. The frequency can be modified by the information-carrying signals that are created when you send data via the modem. The carrier is that irritating "squawking" noise you hear when your modem "talks" to another modem.

case-sensitive   On many of the systems you encounter on the Internet, most notably UNIX, there can 2 be a world of difference between an uppercase and a lowercase letter—a case-senstitive system. Systems such as DOS and VMS are not case sensitive.

catching up   A news reader feature that enables you to quickly handle the mountains of messages that accumulate when you don't attend to your mailing lists. A handy tool to have when you return from a vacation to discover you have hundreds of new mail items.

cc   Carbon copy. Shorthand reference for recipients of copies of an email. There are several schools of thought about sending someone a "carbon copy" of an email message versus listing him or her as a "co-recipient." In short, carbon copy recipients are "secondary" recipients who should be "kept in the loop" on an issue.

If you recall record players and manual typewriters, you may actually remember the days before there was a photocopier in every office. Copies were made at the same time the original document was typed by placing a sheet of

carbon paper between the original sheet and the copy sheet. The carbon copy was sent to the secondary recipient. A quaint idea, but one whose time has come and gone, although the term lives on in the digitial age. *See also* bcc.

CCIRN   *See* **Coordinating Committee for Intercontinental Research Networks**.

CCITT   CCITT stands for the French name of the organization, Comite Consultatif International de Telegraphique et Telephonique. *See also* International Telegraph and Telephone Consultative Committee.

CCL   *See* **Connection Control Language**.

CD-ROM   Compact Disc Read Only Memory. One of a set of competing standards that make use of the large data density of optical disks. CD-ROM technology has come of age in the past couple of years, and may be poised to explode in the near future as the cost of CD-ROM drives drop and CD-ROM titles proliferate. Others predict the CD-ROM boom will be short-lived as high-bandwidth communications may make the technology unnecessary.

cdev   *See* **Control Panel Device**.

cell-switching   A new technology that improves upon X.25 packet-switching and frame relay by bundling data into cells of the same size, thus making the system more efficient and less complex. Part of the Asynchronous Transfer Mode standard.

TIP

Cello for Windows Windows software for browsing World-Wide Web hypertext documents. Also connects to Gopher and WAIS servers. Available by anonymous FTP at `fatty.law.cornell.edu`.

Central Processing Unit (CPU) The part of the computer that does the arithmetic. The CPU contains the arithmetic-logic unit and control unit. In a microcomputer, the CPU is the machine's microprocessor chip. In casual conversations, CPU usually refers to the physical unit—the "box," that contains the chips, or the "brains" of the machine. CPU can mean anything from a mainframe to a laptop.

centralized server *See* **dedicated server**.

Cerf, Vinton G. Designed the protocols (with Robert E. Kahn) that formed the basis of TCP/IP. Currently, president of the Internet Society (ISOC). *See also* Transmission Control Protocol/Internet Protocol.

TIP

CERFnet An Internet service provider primarily serving Southern California, Korea, Mexico, and Brazil, but also the entire U.S. via 800-number access. For information, send email to `help@cerf.net`.

CERN The name of the particle physics laboratory in Geneva Switzerland where the World-Wide Web was created.

CERT *See* **Computer Emergency Response Team**.

CFV *See* **Call For Votes**.

channel 1) A path for signals to travel. In baseband transmission, the wire itelf is the channel. In broadband, there are many channels in a single wire.

2) A conversation group in the Internet Relay Chat (IRC) that is similar to a newsgroup on Usenet or a conference on one of the commercial online providers such as CompuServe or Delphi. The difference is that people on channels send messages that are immediately received by others in the channel, as opposed to the store-and-forward system of newsgroups and conferences.

character Any letter, number, symbol, or punctuation mark that can be stored in one byte. *See also* ASCII.

character length A setting in a terminal emulation program that sets the number of data bits that will be transmitted to make a single character. For example, ASCII characters are 7-bits and require an extra bit for error checking, so the character length setting for ASCII is 8. *Contrast* data bits.

character string A group of alphanumeric elements that cannot be used as numeric operands. "George Washington" is a character string, as is "04-29-59" (because it cannot be used in a numerical operation). *Contrast* numeric string.

character-based interface   An interactive computer system in which the user only sees characters on the screen. There are no icons, scroll bars or other graphical elements. Such an interface can be either a line-oriented or screen-oriented program. In line-oriented programs, what you see on the screen are only the commands you type and the responses from the system you are using. The text appears one line at a time. In screen-oriented programs, you see an organized display that usually fills the entire area of your screen. Many email programs such as PROFS and ALL-IN-1 use this type of interface.

charter   A statement of a newsgroup's topics, its name, and its operational guidelines. A newsgroup's *raison d'être*.

chat   1) In a general sense, chatting involves messaging between nodes on a network. When your computer connects with a host on a LAN, the host sends a login prompt to which your computer responds so that the connection can be made.

2) More specifically, a chat is an online interactive talk program that has been largely replaced by Internet Relay Chat (IRC).

cheapernet   10Base2, thinwire Ethernet. *See also* 10Base2.

checksum   A technique to determine if an error has occurred during data transmission. The sending modem sums up the bytes in the data packet and inserts the result into the packet. The receiving modem opens the packet and performs the same calculation, comparing the result to the original. If the checksums are different, an error has occurred. If the checksums match, there is a high probability (but no guarantee) that no errors occurred. Used by Transmission Control Protocol.

chip   An integrated circuit (IC).

Chooser   A standard Macintosh desk accessory that enables you to select network services. You use the Chooser to select the print driver (for example, LaserWriter) and the specific printer you want, as well as to select AppleShare, and the particular server you want to access.

CIE   *See* **Commercial Internet Exchange**.

CICnet   A midwestern U.S. Internet provider. For information, send email to info@cic.net.

CIJE   *See* **Current Index to Journals in Education**.

CIM   *See* **CompuServe Information Manager**.

circuit-switched network   In this arrangement, the nodes of the network are linked to each other by a dedicated line, point-to-point. Ordinary telephone systems are set up like this, switching circuits to connect callers to each other. Contrast packet-switched network.

CIX   *See* **Commercial Internet Exchange**.

ClariNet   An online international news service that publishes an electronic newspaper made up of national and local news. The chief source of news for ClariNet is UPI. ClariNet is a commercial service— to receive it you must either pay a subscription fee to ClariNet Communications Corporation, or be connected to an Internet provider that has a ClariNet newsfeed. For information about ClariNet, address an email to info@clarinet.com.

CLASS   *See* **Cooperative Library Agency for Systems and Services**.

clear channel   *See* **64K**.

Clearinghouse for Networked Information Discovery and Retrieval (CNIDR)   An organization sponsored by the National Science Foundation (NSF). Its mission is to learn more about the various technologies that search for and retrieve information from networks, such as Gopher, WAIS, and WWW. They encourage developers to make electronic research tools that interoperate. CNIDR provides information about applications as well as source code and bibliographies. CNIDR distributes free-WAIS, a version of WAIS. To contact them, access the World-Wide Web (WWW) and type this URL (Uniform Resource Locator): http://cnidr.org/welcome.html.

client   A program or computer that is able to share the resources (printers, files, programs) of another program or computer called a server. In client/server computing, the client requests services from the server.The client is the machine that is running the client software. It can be either the computer you are sitting in front of or the computer to which you are logged on. In most cases, it is sufficient for you (the user) to think of yourself as the "client." For example, to use FTP you must either access an Internet provider with FTP capability or you need client FTP software on your local computer. There are client software packages for both Macintosh computers and IBM-type PCs. *See also* client/server computing and server.

client/server computing   A model for how computers can share resources in a network. In client/server computing, one component of an application, called the "client," runs on your computer, while another component runs on a "server," a remote computer with files, databases, and programs that you want.

Special software needs to be installed on both the client and the server. The two software parts are complementary. The client makes requests for services such as printing, database processing, and file sharing from the server. Many of the services of the Internet are provided through the client/server model. Gopher, Archie, and WWW are all client/server applications. For example, an Archie client can ask an Archie server to "find this file for me." The server responds to the request by looking for the file and returning with either "here's where you can find the file" or "I couldn't find the file." You can see that in the client/server arrangement, it takes two to tango.

This type of computing requires that both parties have intelligence. You can not have a client/server relationship between a dumb terminal and a host. The latter is called "terminal/host computing." In this model, the terminal sends instructions and the host does all the work.

Client/Server is an evolutionary step-up from terminal/host. It uses network resources more efficiently because two computers are sharing the load. By sharing tasks between clients and servers, less traffic is transmitted around the network and less processing power is used by the client computer.

See also client, host, dumb terminal, server, terminal/host computing.

Clipper Chip A chip containing encryption standards proposed by the National Security Agency (NSA) and endorsed by the Clinton Administration. While Clipper advocates claim that creating a national standard for encryption (such as the Clipper Chip) will make it easier for law enforcement agencies to monitor (presumably illegal) data traffic, Clipper opponents argue that creating a national standard for encryption (such as the Clipper Chip) will make it easier for law enforcement agencies to monitor all data traffic. For more on the Clipper Chip, *see also* the sidebar "Clipping the Wings of Encryption Liberty" next to the entry on encryption on page 64.

CMIP *See* **Common Management Information Protocol**.

CMIS *See* **Common Management Information Services**.

CMOT *See* **Common Management Information Services and Protocol over TCP/IP**.

CMS *See* **Conversational Monitor System**.

CNI *See* **Coalition for Networked Information**.

CNIDR *See* **Clearinghouse for Networked Information Discovery and Retrieval**.

Coalition for Networked Information (CNI) A consortium that includes American Research Libraries, CAUSE, and EDUCOM. The purpose of CNI is to promote scholarship and intellectual productivity through sharing information resources via networks.

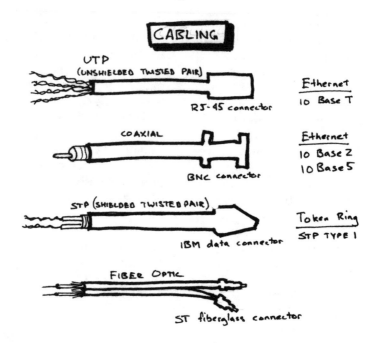

coaxial cable A cable that contains two conductors, one inside the other. They share the same axis, hence co-axial. "Coax," as the techies call it, is the wiring specified for Ethernet 10Base5 (thickwire) and 10Base2 (thinwire) as well as ARCnet. The easiest way to get a look at a piece of coaxial cable is to check out the "cable" over which your cable TV comes into your house and connects to your television—that's coax.

Cola machine Computers are supposed to save labor, right? Well, some Computer Science students at Carnegie Mellon University wired a coke machine to a computer and were able to see if the vending machine was full by sending a message through Internet. And who says computers are making people lazy? Think of all that programming.

collision The result of two devices transmitting at nearly the same time on a network. The message is garbled.

TIP

Colorado Alliance of Research Libraries (CARL) A database that contains abstracts of articles from 10,000 journals made available by the seven member libraries of the alliance. You can access the tables of contents of these magazines for free. You can receive more information—often the full text of the article—through CARL's fee-based UnCover program. For information about CARL, send an email to help@carl.org.

GRAPEFRUIT, LAPDOGS & WHISKERS

If you've noticed a number of Internet tools named after the Archie Comics gang (Archie, Jughead, Veronica) and a plethora of information resources with rather macho names (CARL, ERIC, EDGAR), you might rightfully wonder who names stuff on the Net.

Apparently college students, which would also explain tools with names like Gopher, Finger, and Fetch. Harold McClure, system administrator of Easter Island Network, was once a college student who named a campus computer network: SCAPEGOATS—Student Congress-Approved Publicity Entangled Government-Owned Amendment Tagged System.

McClure decries the current trend of wannabe high-tech firms spouting software and hardware names like DigiMicroCard or TeleGigaCom, and sees the low-tech, goofy Internet names as a refreshing change. A few acronym/names McClure says he would like to see used on the Net include:

LAPDOGS: Local Area Public Database Of Good Stuff

SQUIRM: Super-Quick Utility for Information and Resource Management

WHISKERS: Wide-Horizon Information Standard and Keyed Encryption Regulation Status

GRAPEFRUIT: Global Resource Appliance for Powerful Excavation of Files by Regular Uneducated Information Technicians

TIP

Colorado Supernet A Colorado Internet provider. For information, send email to info@csn.org.

com The domain that includes commercial organizations. Any Internet address with a ".com" tacked onto the end is a commercial entity and thus bears the "com" suffix.

command line The area on a screen—usually indicated by a prompt—where you enter commands for the computer's operating system. DOS, UNIX, and host applications use a command line. This aspect of computing is replaced by graphical elements in a Macintosh or Windows environment.

command mode A state in which anything you type is intepreted as a command to the application you are running, as opposed to inserting text into a document or message. (The latter state is called insert mode.) In a UNIX editor such as vi, you are in command mode by default.

■ ■ ■ ■ ■ ■ ■ ■ **TIP** ■ ■ ■ ■ ■ ■ ■ ■

Commercial Internet Exchange (CIE) An organization that coordinates various service providers that maintain and sell Internet connections. For information about CIE send an email to: `info.cix..org`.

Getting Online to Get Online

Getting connected to the Internet can often be a bit of a chicken-and-the-egg situation. And getting good information about the Internet can also be tough. Email provides good information about the Internet, but you have to be on the Internet (or at least "online" somewhere) to receive that information. Books such as *The Internet Starter Kit for Macintosh* and *The Internet Starter Kit for Windows,* by Adam C. Engst (Hayden Books), are good tools for helping you get on the Internet, as well as good sources of information about the Internet. Another good source is the InterNIC, an organization funded through a grant by the National Science Foundation dedicated to providing information and assistance to Internet users in a number of areas, one of which is network access.

If you're interested in getting access to the Internet (or switching your current status or level of access), the InterNIC can provide you with a current list of commercial access providers or network service providers. (To make things even more confusing, InterNIC calls them "Internet Network Providers.") For a list of companies that will sell you Internet access—even if you just want to shop for lower access rates—call the InterNIC's Referral Desk at 800-444-4345 from 5 A.M. to 7 P.M Pacific time, or send email to `info@internic.net`. The previously listed books offer free trial connection time with a commercial access provider.

■ ■ ■ ■ ■ ■ ■ ■ ■ ■ ■

commercial access providers Organizations that charge a fee to connect to the Internet. Also commonly known as "service providers."

communication program

Software that enables a computer to send signals via a modem to another computer. At its most basic, a communication program does not emulate a terminal. *See also* terminal emulation software.

communication settings

When you use terminal emulation software, there are several variables that you can change to meet the needs of the computer you are communicating with or your own preferences. These settings, or parameters, are normally: baud, parity, duplex, character length, data bits, and stop bits. When in doubt, try using the most common communication settings: 8 data bits, 1 stop bit, and no parity.

Communications Terminal Protocol (CTERM)

A component of the virtual terminal service defined in the DECnet architecture.

Communications Toolbox (CTB)

A built-in feature of Macintosh computer's System 7 operating system that enables a communications program to use different types of pre-configured communications links such as serial, modem, or network connection tools.

■ ■ ■ ■ ■ ■ ■ **TIP** ■ ■ ■ ■ ■ ■ ■ ■

Compact Pro A Macintosh shareware compression program that has a filename extension of "cpt." It was written by Bill Goodman and is widely available throughout the Internet.

compression

A technology that reduces the size of a file. Compression programs are important to network users because, by squeezing files into smaller packages, they reduce online time and expense. Compressors operate by recognizing patterns of data. The percentage of reduction varies. A word processing document may be reduced 70 percent , while a movie (which is already in a compressed form) may only be reduced 14 percent. *Contrast* extract. Also referred to as compacting, shrinking, packing, reducing, stuffing, or zipping.

The normal procedure for transferring a file is to compress it before uploading and to extract (or expand) it after downloading. It is also suggested that you make a copy of the original (uncompressed file) before compressing, because under many compression schemes, the original file is replaced by the compressed version. There is a confusing melange of compression programs. For example, to compress a file named BARGAIN in UNIX, you type: compress BARGAIN. The file will be renamed BARGAIN.Z. To uncompress the file, type uncompress BARGAIN.Z. The file will revert to its orignal name, BARGAIN. There is, in fact, a UNIX compression program called "compress." Its files have the suffix ".Z."

CompuServe With 1.7 million subscribers, CompuServe Information Service (CIS) is the nation's second-largest online service. CompuServe does not have a gateway for Internet services; however, its subscribers can exchange email with Internet users. *See also* Table A.1 "Email Address Formats."

CompuServe Information Manager (CIM) A graphical interface to CompuServe that runs in both Macintosh and Windows environments.

Computer + Science Network (CSNET) A network for institutions doing research in computer science that merged with BITNET in 1989 to form CREN.

Computer Emergency Response Team (CERT) A federally-funded group that addresses computer network security issues. Organized by DARPA following the Internet worm incident of 1988, CERT provides 24-hour technical assistance for security incidents, technical documents, and tutorials. By accessing its server (legally of course), you can obtain information about security tools and recorded break-in attempts on network sites. You can reach it by email at `cert@cert.org` and by telephone at 412-268-7090 (24-hour hotline). *See also* worm and Trojan Horse.

computer-mediated communications Discussion-group systems that enable users to exchange messages via computer networks.

computers In the grand scale of the computer chain-of-being, "micros" are at the bottom, below minicomputer, mainframe, and supercomputer. Personal, laptop, portable, and home computers fall into the "micro" category. There are no standards established for size or performance, but they all have a microprocessor as their CPU.

CONCERT A North Carolina Internet provider. For information, send email to `jrr@concert.net`.

congestion Too much traffic is a problem for information highways as for the concrete kind. In telecommunications, congestion occurs when the capacity of a data communication channel or an online service is exceeded by the amount of data attempting to travel that channel or service.

connect time What the commercial service providers charge you for, or what you may get for "free" if you work for a university, government organization, or large corporation. It's important to note that Internet access isn't ever really "free," and is paid for in one way or another by those who actually use it.

Connection Control Language (CCL)   A scripting language that enables you to control your modem via AppleTalk Remote Access and other communications programs.

connection-oriented communication   A type of application-to-application communication in which a continuous interchange of data is required. There are three phases: make the connection, transfer data, and release the connection. This describes the nature of terminal login sessions and file transfers conducted via Transmission Control Protocol (TCP). *Contrast* connectionless communication.

connectionless communication   A type of application-to-application communication in which data exchange does not require a continuous exchange of data. This is what takes place when a request is made of a database server and the server responds to the request. Packets are independent of each other and may may take different routes. User Datagram Protocol is an example of this. *Contrast* connection-oriented communication.

connections status   Connections to the Internet are either permanent (or persistent) or dial-up (intermittent). Permanent connections are made via high-speed transmission lines. Dial-up connections go through a remote intermediary (what is called an Internet access provider or service provider) that you connect via a modem and ordinary phone lines. If you dial-up, you can connect through a Bulletin Board System (BBS) or an online information service that has a gateway to the Internet. In either of these cases, you would not need any software other than your communications program. You can connect directly to an Internet provider via dial-up as long as your computer has TCP/IP software including either Serial Line Internet Protocol (SLIP) or Point-to-Point Protocol (PPP) capability.

TIP

Consortium for School Networking (CoSN)   A non-profit organization made up of educators throughout the U.S. that focuses on networking issues related to K-12 schools. The aim of CoSN is to make network resources available for students, teachers, and administrators. CoSN works with commercial vendors as well as educational agencies. To contact it, send email to:
`cosn@bitnic.bitnet`.

contention   The result of two devices both signaling their intent to begin transmitting at the same time. This happens in networks such as Ethernet that use Carrier Sense Multiple Access (CSMA) technology. Unresolved contentions would lead to collisions. *See also* Carrier Sense Multiple Access (CSMA) for techniques used to deal with contention.

Control Panel Device (cdev)   One of several Macintosh utility programs that appear as options available under the menu entry Control Panels on the Apple menu under System 7. Among the many cdev's normally found on a Macintosh are Network and MacTCP which are important for setting network connection parameters for your Macintosh. You may also have cdev's from third-party developers for configuring client and SLIP software.

Control Panels   The Macintosh utility found in the Apple menu that you use to customize your Macintosh environment. For Internetters, the Network control panel is particularly important because with it you can choose the network data link (cabling) such as EtherTalk, LocalTalk, TokenTalk, or FDDITalk.

control bus   The wires within a computer that carry control signals for managing the flow of information.

control character   Generally, a nonprinting character that performs or initiates a computer operation. Specifically, an ASCII-character having a value less than 32. For example, backspace is ASCII 8, escape is ASCII 27, and ACK is ASCII 6. Control characters are sent by holding down the Control key and pressing a letter. For example, Control-c terminates a process. The Control key is shown as CTRL or as a caret (^).

control key   The key on your keyboard that is marked CONTROL, control, or CTRL. Also the down arrow on a TRS-80 and the Shift key on a Commodore Vic-20. On screen, you usually see the control key represented by a caret (^).

Conversational Monitor System (CMS)   The user interface to IBM's Virtual Machine operating system. CMS provides a command line to send instructions and make inquiries of mainframe computers.

Cooperative Library Agency for Systems and Services (CLASS)   A California-based Internet provider for member libraries.

Coordinating Committee for Intercontinental Research Networks (CCIRN)   A committee for cooperative planning among North American and European research networking bodies. The executive directors of the U.S. Federal Networking Council (FNC) and the European Association of Research Networks (RARE) co-chair the CCIRN.

copyright The protection given to printed material applies to electronic forms as well—even email. You cannot reuse any copyrighted information or transmit it electronically without permission. The copyright is in effect even if the material does not explicitly say so. When in doubt, ask the publisher. *See also* fair use.

TIP

Corporation for Research and Educational Networking (CREN) An organization formed in 1989 to support BITNET and CSNET users. You can join CREN and receive their newsletter as well as access non-Internet sites. CREN provides a forum for universities and colleges to discuss issues about computers and networks. By Gopher, you can reach CREN at `info.educom.edu` and access a list of all BITNET members.

CoSN *See* **Consortium for School Networking**.

cpt File extension for a Compact Pro file. *See also* Compact Pro.

CPU *See* **Central Processing Unit**.

cracker A programmer who tries to break into a computer, whose motives are malicious and destructive. For whatever reasons, the word cracker has come to mean what hacker formerly meant. This may be because of misuse by reporters, Hollywood scriptwriters, or the general public. *Contrast* hacker.

It's A Conspiracy!

In the `alt.conspiracy` newsgroup, you'll find news, information, opinions, and rumors about a host of topics that are typically ignored or given sloppy coverage by the mainstream media. Contributors to the newsgroup range from those who claim a conspiracy is behind the flawed design of soda can pop-tops to "debunkers" who contend there's no such thing as a conspiracy in the modern world.

If you are interested in an alternative take on current events and recent history, you'll find it among the diverse postings in `alt.conspiracy`. Don't worry about being assaulted with messages about the Kennedy assassination—there's an entirely separate newsgroup (`alt.conspiracy.jfk`) for that topic.

If you can't get enough conspiracy theories in your daily diet of net-browsing, be sure to read Brian Redman's excellent "Conspiracy for the Day," a daily electronic newsletter detailing miscarriages of justice, government chicanery, and other annoying behind-the-scenes machinations. "Conspiracy for the Day" is posted daily to the `alt.conspiracy` newsgroup or is available via email subscription by sending a message to `felix!cfd@cs.du.edu` with the words "subscribe yourname@address" in the body of the message.

In a similar vein is John DiNardo's newsletter, "The People's Spellbreaker," whose motto is "News they never tell you...news they'll never tell you." You'll find the Spellbreaker posted to a number of newsgroups, including `alt.conspiracy`, and as is also the case with Redman's "Conspiracy for the Day," DiNardo encourages the distribution of his bulletins.

CRC *See* **Cyclic Redundancy Check**.

CREN *See* **Corporation for Research and Educational Networking**.

cross-posted Posting the same message to multiple newsgroups or discussion groups by entering more than one group name in the newsgroups line. Easier than sending many separate postings, but cross-posting is not appreciated by some groups.

CrossTalk   (Capitalized.) A proper name for the terminal emulation program with DOS and Windows versions developed by Digital Communications Associates, Inc., Alpharetta, GA.

crosstalk   (Not capitalized.) Electrical interference between pairs of wires in the same cable. Crosstalk can produce errors in data as a result of garbled communications.

CSLIP   Compressed SLIP (Serial Line Internet Protocol). CSLIP compresses IP address information resulting in faster transfer rates.

CSMA   *See* **Carrier Sense Multiple Access**.

CSMA/CA   Carrier Sense Multiple Access with Collision Avoidance. For more information, *see also* Carrier Sense Multiple Access.

CSMA/CD   Carrier Sense Multiple Access with Collision Detection. For more information, *see also* Carrier Sense Multiple Access.

CSNET   *See* **Computer + Science Network**.

CSU/DSU   Channel Service Unit/ Digital Service Unit. A digital conversion device that connects a router to a telephone company channel such as 56K, 64K, or T1.

CTB   *See* **Communications Toolbox**.

CTERM   *See* **Communications Terminal Protocol**.

CWIS   *See* **Campus-Wide Information Server**.

cyber-chat   The cyberspace 24-hour truck-stop—a place to sit down and shoot the breeze with people as you travel down the electronic highway. *See also* talk and Internet Relay Chat.

cyberpork   U.S. government funds that fatten the pockets of information highway businesses, often for producing useless (or nearly useless) products, protocols, standards, tools, or other services.

cyberpunk   The same people who rode on Harleys and wore leathers in previous decades, now jockey around the Internet. For more information, *see also* the following sidebar "Defining Cyberpunk (Not)".

Defining Cyberpunk (Not)

Nobody said being a cyberpunk was easy. Ever since authors like William Gibson and Bruce Sterling began writing speculative fiction on what life in the information-saturated near future may be like (or has become, depending on your time-space perspective), people have been trying to categorize, define, and capitalize on the various

continues

continued

elements of cyberpunk. But cyberpunk is more than virtual reality goggles and decaying technocracies.

Even the folks in the `alt.cyberpunk` aren't positive of exactly what cyberpunk is (or isn't). At least once a week, someone posts a "What is cyberpunk" question, and many queries (such as "Which is more cyberpunkish, *Mondo 2000* or *Wired*?") are so self-analytical they border on self-parody.

Part of the confusion stems from the relative youth of cyberpunk as a literary genre. It's tough to pigeonhole something that's still developing and growing. The mainstream media hasn't helped matters, often lumping everything from "Dr. Who" to the Nintendo Power Glove under the trendy heading of "cyberpunk." Finally, the refusal of cyberpunk creators and aficionados (if, in fact, there is such a clearly defined "community") to be abbreviated, summed up, stamped, packaged, and mass-distributed has confounded those who would "define" cyberpunk. With any luck, things will stay that way for some time to come.

■ ■ ■ ■ ■ ■ ■ ■ ■ ■

Cyberspace   A world in which computers and people coexist. Cyberspace was first envisioned by William Gibson in his science fiction novel, *Necromancer*. Cyberspace is "where" you are when you're online, it's where your money is when it's in the bank, and it's where a lot of corporations expect you to be paying a lot of money to spend time in over the next few years. *See also* Matrix.

Cyclic Redundancy Check (CRC)   A technique that determines if an error has occurred during data transmission. The sending modem performs a calculation and inserts the result into the data block being sent. The receiving modem performs the same calculation and compares the result to the original. If they are different, an error has occurred.

daemon A program that performs a single task and runs in the background on a UNIX system. Daemons wake up periodically to perform the function, and then go back to sleep. There are many different kinds of daemons. You may see it spelled "demon."

daisy chain *See* **bus topology**.

dark fiber Only 0.1 percent of the total capacity of the fiber-optic cabling that has been installed to date is actually being used to transmit anything. The rest is called ominously "dark fiber."

DARPA *See* **ARPA**.

Data Communications (or Circuit-Terminating) Equipment (DCE) Serial-connected devices that establish and control the data link. Dial-up modems are in this class.

Data Encryption Key (DEK) A technology that encrypts messages and signatures. *See also* encryption.

Data Encryption Standard (DES) A security technique defined by the U.S. government. *See also* encryption.

Data Link Layer Layer two of the OSI Reference Model defines the protocols for specifying the assembly and transmission of data packets and frames.

Data Terminal Equipment (DTE) A device that is the source or final destination of data. In this class they are serial-connected devices such as terminals and personal computers.

data In computing, bits that are intelligible to hardware/software.

data bits The number of bits that are transmitted to signify a single character, not counting parity or stop bits. In your communications program, you select either seven or eight bits. *See also* character length.

data block A discrete unit of data as opposed to a data stream which consists of many blocks. Communication between machines and software takes the form of exchanging data blocks. For example, one host will send a data block to another host to confirm delivery of previously sent data.

data bus The wires within a computer that carry information to be transmitted over signal lines.

data link Communications media and equipment that carry data transmissions. This includes the physical components that connect together devices such as cabling and connectors. Sometimes referred to as "link."

data stream Multiple blocks of data that are sent from one device to another. A file that you create in an email program, for example, is sent out as a stream of data from your computer. This is contrasted to a data block which is a discrete unit sent by one device or application to another.

database A structure for storing data in a computer and making the data accessible to a logical search. Databases are generally made up of "records" that are divided into "fields." In a telephone directory database, a person's name, address, and phone number are separate fields. Databases are the gold mines on the Internet—some (for example, DIALOG) are commercial and charge a fee, others are available to the public free of charge. You can think of the Internet as one big database with parts that are highly structured and parts that are not. WAIS (Wide Area Information Server) is a valuable tool for finding what you want.

Datagram Delivery Protocol (DDP) A network layer protocol that enables addressing of AppleTalk datagrams over an AppleTalk network. The AppleTalk Network layer protocol accepts data from the layers above it and breaks the data into packets for transmission over the network. DDP communicates between two sockets on the network and ensures the integrity of the data delivered.

datagram A packet of information, consisting of data and a header that is placed within network frames for delivery over the network. The datagram's header shows the source, destination, the type of data it contains, and its relation to any other datagrams being sent. This header information enables the data to be transported from router to router to its destination. Datagrams are unique to the particular protocol being applied.

In TCP/IP, a "datagram" is the packet into which the Internet Protocol (IP) places the segments delivered by the Transmission Control Protocol (TCP). Datagrams may arrive out of sequence or damaged in delivery. Such problems are resolved by TCP. *See also* frame, and packet.

dd File extension for a DiskDoubler compressed file.

DDCMP *See* **Digital Data Communications Message Protocol**.

DDN *See* **Defense Data Network**.

DDN NIC *See* **Defense Data Network Network Information Center**.

DDP *See* **Datagram Delivery Protocol**.

DEC *See* **Digital Equipment Corporation**.

DECnet A suite of proprietary networking protocols developed by Digital Equipment Corporation for use on VAX/VMS and PDP-11 computers, PCs, and other computers. Versions of DECnet are available for Macintosh from Digital and Thursby Software Systems. These protocols are not compatible with the Internet.

DECnet tunnel A technique used by AppleTalk for VMS and DECnet that encapsulates AppleTalk datagrams within DECnet packets for delivery over a DECnet link.

DECnet/DNA The series of network protocols defined by Digital Computer, Inc. DNA, or Digital Network Architecture, that contains the definitions of the protocols. DECnet is Digital's implementation of DNA.

dedicated An adjective applied to equipment that is reserved for a single function or task (for example, a computer that is set up as a file server). The term is also applied to single-minded people who slave over BBSs, SIGs, or dictionaries.

dedicated line A telephone line that is used exclusively for telecommunications. Synonymous with leased line.

deep hack A state of mind reached by hackers who have been spelunking deeper and deeper into the Net for hours on end. Deep hack status is marked by the eyes glazing over or rolling back in the head and a complete lack of acknowledgment of the outside world.

default A setting that is in effect when you start up a computer or open an application, until you change it.

default route An entry in a routing table that shows where to direct packets that have an address that is not explicitly given in the table.

default zone The AppleTalk default zone for a device when initially placed on an extended (Phase 2) network.

Defense Data Network (DDN) The U.S. military's all-encompassing global communications network that includes some networks that are connected to the Internet and some that are not. The DDN connects U.S. military bases and contractors to the Internet for nonsecure communications. The DDN is managed by the Defense Information Systems Agency.

Defense Data Network Network Information Center (DDN NIC) Provides a variety of services for the DDN that includes assigning Internet addresses and Autonomous System numbers, administering the root domain, and providing information. Sometimes referred to as "the NIC."

Defense Information Systems Agency (DISA) The government agency that manages the DDN, including the MILNET. Formerly called the Defense Communications Agency (DCA).

DEK *See* **Data Encryption Key**.

TIP

Delphi Information Service A commercial online information service owned by News America Corporation. In addition to its own package of services that include message forums, Delphi has an Internet gateway available through a connection with the New England Academic and Research Network (NEARNET). The Internet services include FTP, Telnet, Gopher, Usenet, and Internet Relay Chat.

TIP

Demon Internet Services A UK Internet provider. For information, send email to `internet@demon. co.uk`. **DES** *See* **Data Encryption Standard**.

dial-up To use communications software and a modem to call up another computer and connect for a limited-time session. To access the Internet through dialing up, you can call a service provider directly and access services via a BBS-style interface, connect to an intermediary such as Delphi or America Online, or you can directly connect by using software that uses SLIP or PPP (which allow a more graphically-oriented approach to surfing the Internet). *Contrast* dedicated line.

TIP

DIALOG Information Retrieval Services A commercial online database service in operation since 1972. It has more than 400 different databases and hundreds of millions of records from journal abstracts to corporate financial statements. If you are connected to the Internet, you can connect to DIALOG. To contact DIALOG, telnet to `dialog.com`.

digest A single file with a bunch of individual messages stuffed into it.

digestified A mailing list or newsgroup posting that has been placed into a file with other postings.

Digital Data Communications Message Protocol A DECnet data link protocol the enables point-to-point linking of nodes in either asynchronous or synchronous modes.

Digital Equipment Corporation (DEC) Producer of the VAX line of computers and the VMS operating system. Also known as "Digital."

digital Said of a device that records or transmits discontinuous pieces or bits—as opposed to an analog device that processes continuous variations. A person singing, a piece of quartz vibrating, a movie image—when represented digitally, all input is reduced to numbers. The major advantage of digital over analog is the control and accuracy it provides. Compact discs and laser disks are digital. A modem converts the digital signals coming through your computer into the analog waves needed to transmit over phone lines, and performs the conversion in reverse when receiving information over the phone.

directed information Data that is intended for a specific recipient usually in the form of personal email exchanges. *Contrast* undirected information.

Directory Access Protocol An X.500 protocol that defines how a Directory User Agent (DUA) communicates with a Directory System Agent (DSA).

Directory System Agent (DSA) In the X.500 Directory Service, this software handles queries about directory information from Directory User Agents (DUA).

Directory User Agent (DUA) In the X.500 Directory Service, this software enables a user (a person or software routine) to access the X.500 Directory Service and make inquiries.

directory Table of contents of the files contained on a disk. A directory can show file name, file size, date and time created, file type, and author. Some directories also show the privileges applied to the file.

directory service A source of network addresses, usernames, hosts and services. *See also* white pages.

DISA *See* **Defense Information Systems Agency**.

disable To make inactive without necessarily shutting off. Has the effect of putting into neutral, as opposed to shutting down completely.

A Kinder, Gentler Vocabulary

It's no wonder computers are prone to glitches and snafus from time to time. "Disable" isn't the most polite way of saying "deactivate" or "make neutral." Just think about what your computer goes through in an average day.

You arrive at work and boot up. There are a few files left over from yesterday taking up precious hard drive space, so you expunge them. You log on to the Net and capture a text file and check your mail. There is a flame waiting for you, to which you respond. Unfortunately, your email software hangs and the message gets bounced. You worry that the problem may be a virus, so you execute your disinfectant routine. When finished, you pack, stuff, or zip the software and file it away. You wonder what kind of hacker or cracker might have created such a virus, and just when you're finishing up for the day, your system crashes.

discussion group Online encounters with your own kind. In discussion groups, participants exchange messages about particular topics. There are many varieties and formats. *See also* mailing list, and Usenet news groups.

Disk Operating System (DOS) Officially known as MS-DOS (Microsoft Disk Operating System), DOS is a computer operating system that gives the user a command line to interact with the CPU. Originally developed by Microsoft, DOS is now found in several varieties and is used on IBM and IBM-type computers. DOS is a single-user operating system as distinguished from NETBIOS, which accommodates multiple users. Reactions to the complexity of DOS commands lead to the graphical interface of Macintosh, NeXT, and Windows operating systems.

disk drive A storage device that retains data by magnetizing small regions on the surface of a disk. While the term "disk drive" most commonly refers to an internal hard disk drive, it also can apply to a floppy drive, external hard disk, or other variety of drive such as a magneto-optical or Syquest-style drive. Virtually all of the files available via the Internet are stored on disk drives.

disk server Software that enables your computer to use a partition of another computer's hard disk as though it were a local disk drive. A disk server does not let anyone share the file in the partition, as opposed to a file server, which does enable file sharing.

diskette Whatever you call it: floppy, micro cassette, micro-floppy, floppette, disk...it's either a 5-1/4" square or a 3-1/2" square that you stick into the slot of your computer.

Distinct TCP/IP for Windows Software that provides a Windows interface for FTP and telnet. With it, you can access the Internet via a LAN or dial-in using SLIP or PPP. Developed by Distinct Corporation.

Distributed Computing Environment (DCE) A set of programming interfaces, conventions, and server functions adopted by the Open Software Foundation (OSF) for distributing applications across diverse networks.

distributed computing A method of distributing applications transparently across diverse networks.

distributed database Collections of data residing on different hosts that can be accessed by the user as though they were allocated on a single host. The Domain Name System is a distributed database because it can translate network names into IP addresses by searching a number of different hosts.

distributed server A network technology that enables computers to share drives and printers across the network while still being able to run their own applications. The server functions, such as file storage and printing, usually occur in the background. Also called "peer-to-peer network." *Contrast* server network. *See also* peer-to-peer.

distribution list A roster of usernames and email addresses that are assigned an alias, for example, "Headquarters." When you address a message to the distribution list "Headquarters," all the people on the list receive the message.

DIX Digital, Intel, and Xerox. *See also* Ethernet.

DIX Ethernet *See* **Ethernet**.

DLIST A list of Internet service providers that offer dedicated-line and dialup connections.

DNS *See* **Domain Name System**.

DoD *See* **U.S. Department of Defense**.

Domain Name System A set of distributed databases that contain Internet Protocol (IP) addresses (for example, 123.456.666.123) and

their corresponding domain names (for example, orion.oac.uci.edu). Instead of one computer containing the names of all the hosts on the Internet, name servers are spread around the network. If a local server does not recognize a name and address, it will communicate with another server to get the information. The reason for keeping two sets of names is to enable users to use "friendly" English-language names, instead of a mysterious string of numbers. *See also* Fully Qualified Domain Name, and IP address.

■ ■ ■ ■ ■ ■ ■ ■ **TIP** ■ ■ ■ ■ ■ ■ ■ ■

domain One of the main partitions of the Internet. A domain is the highest level of the Domain Name System naming hierarchy and forms the right-most part of an Internet address. There are a number of various three-character "descriptive" domains:

Domain	Description
edu	educational
mil	military
org	miscellaneous organizations
gov	government
com	commercial
net	network resources

continues

continued

Domain	Description

There are also two-character "locative" domains representing 100 countries. There are many you would expect to see:

uk	United Kingdom
ca	Canada

And some you may not expect to see:

cx	Christmas Island
aq	Antarctica
kn	Saints Kitts and Nevis

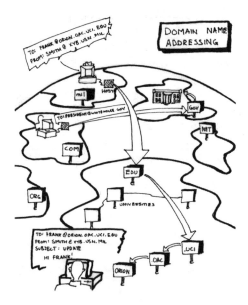

network to which the computer is attached; the sub-domain (for example, a university—not all addresses have a sub-domain) and the Internet domain. This information follows the @ sign and the username to make up an Internet address. A domain name reads from the specific to the general. Domain names are translated into IP addresses by the Domain Name System. More accurately (but less commonly) called the "hierarchical name."

■■■■■■■■■■■■■■■■■■■■■

DOS *See* **Disk Operating System**.

dot address or dotted decimal notation or dotted quad Other names for the standard IP address. So called because the numbers have periods (or "dots") between each group.

■■■■■■■■ **TIP** ■■■■■■■■

domain name A multi-part description made up of (reading from left to right): the name of the computer on which the user's account resides; the group or

download Moving data from a remote (usually larger) computer to a local (usually smaller) computer. In the user's point of view, downloading means to receive data from another computer. *Contrast* upload.

downstream Usenet news flows from computer to computer. The computer receiving the news from your host computer is said to be downstream. *Contrast* upstream.

downtime When machines or networks are inoperative, they are "down." Downtime is the period during which you can't log on.

driver Software that enables your computer to communicate with a peripheral hardware device such as a printer.

DS1 Digital Signal Level 1. An AT&T specification defining frames for T-1 lines.

DS3 Digital Signal Level 3. An AT&T specification defining frames for T-3 lines.

DSA *See* **Directory System Agent**.

DSO Digital Signal Level 0 (64K).

DTE *See* **Data Terminal Equipment**.

DUA *See* **Directory User Agent**.

dumb terminal An input-output device that sends keystrokes to a computer and displays data on a video screen. A terminal is considered "dumb" because it lacks software and a storage area for

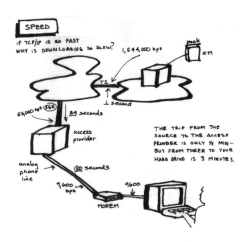

data—both of which are found only on the computer to which it is connected. Before the era of microprocessors and personal computers, a terminal was the only game in town for human beings to directly interact with computers. When you login to a mainframe computer to use Internet services (or use a simple terminal to access a library's holdings or a campus-wide information system), your personal computer is imitating a dumb terminal, such as a Digital VT100 or an IBM 3270. You may say this is reverse evolution.

duplex Transmission of signals in two directions at the same time. *See also* half duplex, full duplex, and simplex.

Dying Child Postcard *See* **urban legend**.

dynamic adaptive routing Automatic directing of network traffic based on an analysis of current network conditions.

dynamic node addressing A
technique enabling nodes to
automatically select unique network addresses. Used on AppleTalk
networks. Contrasted with domain
addressing used in TCP/IP in which
computer node addresses are
assigned centrally and maintained
on a single host computer. Used
on TCP/IP and DECnet networks.
See also Domain Name System.

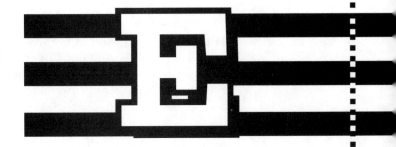

E-journal An electronic publication. Typically found in academic circles, an e-journal is a regularly published journal either made available in electronic form or published solely in electronic form. The advantage for publishing academic findings in an e-journal (rather than or in addition to an e-journal) include wider distribution, lower cost of retrieval, faster delivery time, and more searchable format.

email Electronic mail. *See also* mail for more information.

email address *See* **mail address**.

E-text A text document in electronic form. An e-text may take the form of a short pamphlet, a Read Me file or brief note.

E-zine A magazine (or "fanzine") published in electronic form. Scores of e-zines are published on a regular (and sporadic) basis across the Internet with topics ranging from science-fiction-inspired poetry to the angst of living in the digital age.

The Evolution Has Been Digitized

Not long after the arrival of Macintosh, PageMaker and the laser printer, a revolution called "desktop publishing" took the printing and publishing industries by storm. The result is a quantum leap forward in the way books and magazines are created and published.

At least as important (and perhaps more so) as the technological revolution was the resultant explosion in small press publications. While the mainstream magazine market suffered micro-cycles of feast and famine throughout the late 80s and early 90s, the world of small press magazines (or "fanzines") grew exponentially.

continues

continued

These fanzines started as hobby-oriented special-interest publications, often centered around cults or enclaves of fandom, like "Star Trek" or "Dungeons and Dragons." But before long, it seemed like literally everyone with a laser printer and a photocopier was producing his own magazine.

Fanzines (now called simply "zines") have undergone another revolution, making the leap from slow-moving, expensive paper entities to boundless dispatches roaming the electronic ether. While paper zines continue to proliferate, electronic zines (or "e-zines") are the real growth market for unfettered self-expression.

Some e-zines are sophisticated digital reflections of the best that paper magazines have to offer. Others are crude text files featuring the wild ramblings of a voice that demands to be heard. No paper newsstand can offer titles as out-of-the-ordinary as "Practical Anarchy Online" or "Unplastic News." Electronic distribution means access to a potential audience of millions, at virtually no cost to the publisher or reader.

You can download the passion, expertise, individuality, and energy of scores of e-zines from a number of sites throughout the Net. The best place to start is by checking out the `alt.zines` newsgroup. An updated list of e-zines is posted there (and to a number of other relevant newsgroups) every three weeks. For a copy of the latest list, you can also check out the `/pub/johnl/zines/` directory via anonymous FTP at `ftp.netcom.com`.

TIP

eWorld Unlike the AppleLink service for developers and Apple specialists, eWorld is an online service created by Apple Computer and aimed at rank-and-file computer users. Based on America Online's software, eWorld is a highly graphical service offering brand-name areas run by information providers known as "publishers."

EARN *See* **European Academic and Research Network**.

EBCDIC *See* **Extended Binary Coded Decimal Interchange Code**.

echo The return of a transmitted signal to its source. When interacting with a remote computer, what you type is received by the other computer and sent back to your screen. This is called "local echo." Remote echo is a copy of the data received by the remote system, returned to the sending system and displayed on the screen.

Is There An Echo In Here? Echo In Here?

Since most host computers and BBSs automatically echo the characters you send, you don't have to turn on your terminal emulator's "Local Echo" feature. In other words, keep your communication software set to "echo off." Sometimes you will need to turn on echo when you are communicating in real time with another personal computer, or when you're using some information services such as GEnie.

The echo is a toggle. If you see no characters, change the current setting. If you see double characters (wwhhiicchh wwiill llookk lliikkee tthhiiss), change the current setting.

TIP

EcoNet A bulletin board system involving organizations and individuals concerned about environmental issues. To send email to someone on the EcoNet, address it to: `username@igc.org`.

EDGAR A database on the transactions and financial status of corporations that is maintained by the U.S. Security Exchange Commission (SEC). It is available on the Internet.

editor A program that enables you to create, edit, and save documents. By today's word processing standards, the typical editors (also commonly known as "text editors") used in the Internet are rudimentary. Internet text editors boast few of the features users of WordPerfect and Microsoft Word have come to expect. You can forget about tables, pictures, and fancy fonts. Editors will put words on the computer screen for you, but to re-write or correct typos, you need to issue commands. For the most part, editing programs you're likely to see on the Internet run on UNIX systems, but sometimes you'll encounter editors on VAX and IBM mainframes as well. There is a built-in UNIX mail editor that leaves many people howling for anything even a little bit better. In UNIX mail, for example, you must type a period (.) on a single line to indicate the end of the message. You can substitute other editors such as vi, emacs, ee, ex, and joe by evoking them with the tilde escape command.

EDT An editor used in Delphi and VMS.

edu The domain that includes educational institutions, for instance: `sunsite@unc.edu`.

Educational Resources Information Center (ERIC) A service providing an online database containing bibliographic information and abstracts from hundreds of journals from education, management, health, and technology. The database itself is called the "ERIC Clearinghouse on Information Resources" and is located at Syracuse University. You can reach a gopher server at: `ericir.syr.edu`.

EDUCOM An organization that supports colleges and universities in deploying computers in classrooms and laboratories. They are advocates of the National Research and Education Network (NREN). To contact them, send an email to: `inquiry@bitnic.educom.edu`.

ee A UNIX editor that uses Control-key commands and a pop-up menu. ee is not rich in features, but it is relatively easy-to-use. It is not a full-screen editor, and it was not named after the poet, e.e. cummings.

EFF *See* **Electronic Frontier Foundation**.

EFLA Extended Four-Letter Acronym. *See also* TLA.

EGP *See* **Exterior Gateway Protocol**.

EIA *See* **Electronics Industries Association**.

EIA/TIA-568 A document that defines a universal building wiring standard upon which telecommunications systems and LANs are based. It was authored by the American National Standards Institute, Electronics Industry Association, and Telecommunications Industry Association.

ELAP *See* **EtherTalk Link Access Protocol**.

Electronic Bulletin Board *See* **Bulletin Board Service**.

Electronic Frontier Foundation (EFF) An organization that promotes freedom on the electronic highways. Founded by computer industry luminary Mitch Kapor and Grateful Dead lyricist John Perry Barlow, the EFF is active in shaping legislation affecting civil rights in cyberspace. While some have puzzled over exactly what an "electronic frontiersman" might do (not to mention what he'd look like), the EFF claims a number of members from among the inhabitants of cyberspace. Members examine the effect that computers have on society, especially the social and legal issues of communication and the dissemination of information through networks. For more information, send a request to `info@eff.org` or check out the EFF archives at `ftp.eff.org`.

electronic mail The electronic exchange of messages between individuals via computers. *See also* mail.

Electronics Industries Association (EIA) A professional organization that sets standards for the electronics industry.

elm A full-screen UNIX mail program that organizes incoming and outgoing mail. It is relatively easy to use and has many features. It lists common commands at the bottom of the screen. The main screen is called the "Index window."

emacs A UNIX full-screen editor. In addition to enabling you to create and edit documents, emacs provides some of the functionality of a UNIX shell because you can read and manage mail, read

Usenet news, and create macros. emacs have a reputation for being powerful, but difficult to use.

emoticons Emotion icons. *See also* smileys.

emulation *See* **terminal emulation**.

encapsulation The process of incorporating information from different protocol layers into a single unit that can be transported across networks. When data is sent out, the topmost protocol layer adds information in the form of a header and passes it along to the next lower layer, which in turn adds information. In TCP/IP, a data stream is sent by a computer. TCP breaks up the stream and puts the bits together with a header into a segment. IP then puts the segment together with a header into a datagram. The physical layers then put the datagrams into frames to be transported. On the receiving end, the process takes place in the reverse order.

encoding A method of representing binary digits ("0s" and "1s") so that the transceivers at both ends of a communication path send and receive accurate data.

encryption A procedure that makes the contents of a file unintelligible to anyone not authorized to read it. Encryption is a standard network security technique. *See also* Data Encryption Standard.

Clipping the Wings of Encryption Liberty

It's not a news flash to most people that the civil liberties promised to Americans in the local town square don't necessarily extend to cyberspace. Clearly, the tools and technologies we use to express and communicate ideas and information has outstripped the laws and social conventions that govern the use of those tools.

Perhaps no other issue has raised the ire of Internet users than the Clipper Chip and SKIPJACK encryption scheme. Endorsed in February of 1994 by the Clinton Administration as a means for standardizing U.S. encryption technologies, the Clipper Chip has been widely and robustly criticized as the digital incarnation of Orwell's Big Brother.

If adopted as the national standard for encryption technology, the Clipper Chip would allow government agencies to monitor virtually any form of electronic communication, including electronic mail, fax transmissions, and voice telephone calls.

The editors of *Wired* magazine warn that if the Clipper/SKIPJACK standards are adopted and implemented, "we could shortly find ourselves under a government with the automated ability to log the time, origin, and recipient of every call and email message, to monitor our most private communication, to track our physical whereabouts continuously, and to keep better account of our financial transactions than we do—all without a warrant."

The Electronic Frontier Foundation's John Perry Barlow has warned that "trusting the government with your privacy is like trusting a Peeping Tom to install your window blinds." Jerry Berman, executive director of the EFF has asserted that "the Clipper Chip marks a dramatic new effort on the part of the government to prevent us from being able to engage in truly private conversations."

For more information on the Clipper Chip and related legislation and policy decisions, send email containing the words "send clipper/index" on a single line inside the message body to: infobot@wired.com.

■ ■ ■ ■ ■ ■ ■ ■ ■ ■

end-to-end The type of connection that exists between two computers that are communicating (sending and receiving) directly with each other. *Contrast* store-and-forward.

end-user Anyone who uses a computer. Tech-support personnel often use the term with sarcastic derision to refer to mere mortals who simply use computers for everyday work.

enterprise computing A corporate network connecting different types of computers that are likely to be running a variety of operating systems and network protocols. Enterprise computing seeks to preserve a corporation's investment in heterogeneous hardware by enabling all platforms to interoperate.

ERIC *See* **Educational Resources Information Center**.

error control Various methods of checking the reliability of data being transmitted. *See also* checksum, parity, CRC, V.42bis, and MNP.

Ethernet A set of LAN cabling specifications and protocols developed by Xerox, Intel, and Digital (sometimes referred to as "DIX"). Ethernet supports both thick and thinwire coaxial cable as well as unshielded twisted-pair wiring. Ethernet bandwidths range from 2 to 10 Mbps. Computers using TCP/IP frequently connect to the Internet via an Ethernet LAN. The main difference between Ethernet and Token Ring is how multiple nodes access a single channel. Ethernet nodes contend for access (via CSMA/CD), whereas Token Ring nodes wait for permission (token passing). Defined in IEEE 802.3.

Ethernet meltdown A catastrophic expression describing a minor event in the life of a network. A "meltdown" occurs when misdirected packets begin to overwhelm or "saturate" an Ethernet network. A jammed-up LAN does not a Chernobyl make.

EtherTalk Apple's implementation of AppleTalk protocols on Ethernet. EtherTalk places the Datagram Delivery Protocol (DDP) datagrams into Ethernet frames.

EtherTalk Link Access Protocol (ELAP) The AppleTalk Data link protocol that runs on Ethernet.

etx File extension for a setext file.

Eudora A Macintosh email client program that enables you to use POP and SMTP (common protocols for handling electronic mail traffic) to access the Internet. Available by anonymous FTP at: `sumex-aim.stanford.edu`.

EUnet A European Internet provider. For information, send email to: `glenn@eu.net`.

European Academic and Research Network (EARN) A network of European academic and research institutions that connect to Bitnet for electronic mail and file transfers.

even parity *See* **parity**.

execute To run a program. In directory listings, shown as an "x" next to the file or directory name. *See also* privileges.

expire To automatically remove postings by a certain date to conserve space.

Extended Binary Coded Decimal Interchange Code (EBCDIC) IBM's system for translation between characters and an eight-bit code. EBCIDC represents up to 256 characters, providing in addition to ASCII's 128 character-set, characters to draw lines and boxes, special symbols such as pi (π), international punctuation, and scientific notation. EBCDIC also allows base-10 calculations with greater accuracy in binary circuits and is used by IBM mainframes. Due to its proprietary nature, EBCDIC did not catch on. Even though ASCII is not as sophisticated, it is more widely used, especially on the Internet. Pronounced EB-se-dik. *See also* ASCII.

extension *See* **filename extension**.

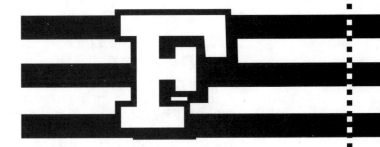

fair use Using copyrighted material in a legal manner. Fair use generally means you can quote or abstract limited portions of a work. This does not allow you to use quoted material for commercial purposes. If you use it for yourself, fine—which is also what you'll get if you transmit it to others without permission. Since copyright issues haven't been fully explored and defined on the Internet, it's best to err on the side of safety and courtesy and get permission before using something that might be copyrighted. *See also* copyright.

FAQ Frequently Asked Question file. In your Internet travels, you'll often come across this abbreviation. Network servers, newsgroups, and mailing lists regularly distribute a FAQ file with typical questions and answers. It's intended to address one of those vicious cycles in life: as a beginner, you nag an expert with a million questions until you become an expert and then a greenhorn comes along to nag you with the same questions. If you're new to a group, break the cycle and consult the FAQ posting before asking questions. Odds are, you'll find the answer to your question (and tons of other useful info). You'll save yourself and the administrators a lot of time.

Says Who?

It's rare that you've got something to say about anything important that someone else hasn't already said, and probably more eloquently and succinctly. The Net is a living testament to this disappointing realization, not only in its infinite postings by experts and authorities on everything from biochemistry to Ren & Stimpy cartoons, but also as a great source of time-tested quips and quotations by famous folks on all matters of import. Enough great quotes lurk in the hidden corners of the Internet to make even John Bartlett blush.

The first place to visit in search of great quotes is the `alt.quotations` newsgroup. Dedicated to exchanging, archiving, indexing, verifying, and discussing quotes of all kinds, the newsgroup is full of great quotes and information on other quote sources on the Net.

The `alt.quotation` newsgroup's Frequently Asked Questions (FAQ) file, which is copyrighted Jonathan Monsarrat (`jgm@cs.brown.edu`)

continues

continued

and Michael Moncur (mgm@world.std.com), explores the nuances of what makes for a great quote.

To paraphrase from the alt.quotation's FAQ file, good quotes should meet a few simple criteria to be immortalized in the quotation archives: they should be short (five lines or less—six lines is really an excerpt), they should be exact (anything other than an exact quote is just paraphrasing), they should have an attribution unless they are well-known anonymous quotes, they should be from someone famous (not your cousin or college roommate), they should mean something, and they shouldn't be one-liner jokes or cliches.

If a quote is classic enough to meet these stringent standards, it will be added to a list of quotations archived and available via anonymous FTP at wilma.cs.brown.edu in the pub/alt.quotations/archive/ directory.

There are dozens of smaller FTP sites devoted to archiving quotes only from a particular individual. While they are too numerous to mention here, you can start your celebrity quote searches in the varioius directories of the FTP archives at quartz.rutgers.edu and cathouse.org.

As Mae West almost said, "Why don't you FTP up and download me sometime?"

■■■■■■■■■■

FARNET A non-profit corporation that seeks to facilitate research and education through the use of computer networks.

fast packet *See* **ATM**.

FDDI *See* **Fiber Distributed Data Interface**.

Federal Information Exchange (FIX) A connection between various U.S. Government networks and the Internet.

Federal Information Processing Standards (FIPS) A Department of Defense document that de-scribes the U.S. government's policy regarding computer networking and the planned transition from TCP/IP to OSI standards. *See also* Government Open Systems Interconnection Profile (GOSIP).

Federal Networking Council (FNC) An organization of representatives from various federal agencies that coordinates how the federal network is used and developed, particularly TCP/IP networks and the Internet. Representatives include Department of Defense (DoD), Department of Energy (DoE), Defense Advanced Research

Projects Agency (DARPA), National Science Foundation (NSF), and National Aeronautics and Space Administration (NASA).

feed A connection to a source of mail and news.

Fetch Macintosh FTP software developed at Dartmouth that retrieves files. Fetch is freeware for educational and nonprofit users and shareware for others. Available by anonymous FTP at: sumex-aim.stanford.edu.

Fiber Distributed Data Interface (FDDI) A system that provides a backbone for metropolitan area networks. It is built upon two rings of fiber optic cabling to carry data. Typically, LANs are connected to the FDDI by routers that are attached to the primary ring. The secondary ring is for backup and gives FDDI high reliability. FDDI can run 60 miles of cabling and has a signaling rate of 80M bits of data per second.

fiber optic cable A transmission medium that carries pulses of light over strands of glass. Fiber optic cables can carry hundreds of millions of bits per second over thousands of miles. Since the glass fibers are carrying light, they do not receive outside interference and do not lose appreciable strength. Fiber optic transmission therefore produces fewer errors than copper wiring, but is much more expensive.

Data is transmitted in the form of light pulses that represent logical bits (1s and 0s). The sending end is a laser light source that converts electrical signals into light and the receiving end converts the light back into electrical signals.

A fiber optic cable contains two glass strands because light signals only pass in one direction. Each strand, or fiber, is covered in a sheath made of Kevlar and plastic.

field A segment of a database record that is intended for specific information. In an individual email account record, for example, there would typically be a username field, a password field, a host name field, and so forth.

File Transfer Protocol (FTP) 1) The TCP/IP protocol that enables you to copy files from one machine to another on the Internet. With FTP, you can also manage files by renaming or deleting them. FTP was designed to solve several problems encountered with transferring files between different systems. FTP manages to resolve the differences in file naming conventions, directory rules, host access restrictions, and file formats. FTP can be used by interactive users or applications. It transfers both ASCII and binary files.

FTP enables you to transfer files from your computer to a host, from a host to your computer, or between hosts. It is mainly used in the second way, namely, to copy files from a remote host to the one you are logged on to (the local host).

2) The UNIX application program that uses the protocol.

3) The command that evokes the program.

4) The act of transferring a file using FTP, as in, "You can FTP that file from Stanford's archives on the Internet."

For more information and an example of using FTP, *see also* anonymous FTP.

FTP Commands

FTP Command	Description
ascii	Sets up an ASCII (7-bit text) transfer
binary	Sets up an (8-bit) binary transfer
cd directoryname	Changes the directory on the remote host
close	Ends the session and returns you to the FTP prompt
dir filename destination	Displays the contents of the current directory
get remote-file	Downloads the file to your local host
hash	Displays a # every time a block is transferred
help command	Shows help for the command
lcd directoryname	Sets default directory on your local host
ls filename destination	Displays a short version of the directory
mget file-list	Downloads several files at one time to your local host
mput file-list	Uploads several files at one time to the remote host
open address	Makes a connection to the remote host
prompt	Toggles whether MGET or MPUT prompts you for confirmation of individual files
put (or copy or send)	Uploads a file to the remote host
pwd	Shows the name of the current directory on the remote host. (PWD stands for "Print working directory")
quit	Closes the connection and exits you from FTP

file A group of data that belongs together, such as a letter or a spreadsheet, typically on magnetic media.

file server A computer that is intended for the storage of files that are shared by multiple users across a network. Usually file servers are dedicated devices, that is, they are not available for any other function. There are, however, file servers that are not dedicated. On some networks, a workstation can perform file server tasks in addition to other functions, including desktop applications such as word processors, spreadsheets, or databases.

file site Internet computers that hold files that are accessible to practically everyone. Also known as an "archive site" or "FTP site."

file transfer To move a copy of a file from one computer to another over a network. The term is somewhat misleading because a copy of the file is transferred, not the file itself.

file-locking Reserving a shared file for the first user who opens it and locking out other users. This data management technique maintains the integrity of data entry because it prevents the file from being altered by more than one person at a time.

filename extension A three-letter suffix that follows a filename that shows the type of file. DOS and UNIX environments require extensions. Although the Macintosh does not normally require a filename extension, its applications do have extensions that, when crossing network boundaries, are used to identify the originating application. Refer to table below for common filename extensions.

Filename Extensions

Extension	Program / Format
ARC	A DOS archiving format
cpt	Compact Pro (Mac compression)
dd	DiskDoubler (Mac compression)
etx	Setext
gif	Pictures in graphic interchange format
gz	gzip compression program
HQX	BinHex
jpeg	JPEG-compressed image
mpeg	MPEG-compressed animation

continues

continued

Filename Extensions

newsrc	The file created by UNIX newsreaders showing newsgroups and messages
pit	Macintosh PackIt (compression)
pkg	AppleLink Package (compression)
sea	Macintosh self-extracting archive
sit	StuffIt (compression)
tar	UNIX tar archive files (compression)
txt	text file
uu, .uud, .uue	uuencoded file formats
x	SuperDisk self-extracting archive More DiskSpace compressed file
Z	UNIX compress program
z	GNU Zip compressed file
ZIP	ZIP compressed file

TIP

filter (Noun) Software that converts one file format into another. (Verb) To exclude unwanted data in a transmission. Many email programs offer the capability to filter email messages to specific directories based on keywords in the message's header, subject line, or body, which is an especially helpful trick if you read and respond to dozens of email messages daily.

TIP

finger A UNIX utility that enables you to find out who has an account on an Internet computer as well as information about the other users. Finger provides more information than whois. It typically displays the full name, last time the person logged in, idle time, terminal time, and terminal location. Sometimes users create plan and project files. If used, finger will be able to display those files as

well. Finger is found on most Internet servers; although some servers have chosen to disable finger to protect the privacy of their users. For example, you cannot use finger to get information about a Delphi user. The format of the command is:
`%finger username@host`
where username is the full name or login id and host is the name of the computer.

TIP

Finger for the Macintosh
Macintosh finger software. Available by anonymous FTP at `sumex-aim.stanford.edu`. Finger for the Macintosh enables Mac users to execute finger commands using a graphical interface rather than the standard command-line method.

FIPS *See* **Federal Information Processing Standards**.

FirstSearch Catalog *See* **Online Computer Library Center**.

FIX *See* **Federal Information Exchange**.

flame An expression of displeasure from another user, which can range from finger-wagging to total thermonuclear war. Such verbal conflagrations are usually heralded in the subject by "FLAME ON!" One who engages in these email fisticuffs is called a "flamer." Such outbursts are to be expected on a system employing user-enforced etiquette. Transgressions can be looked upon as the equivalent of putting the fork on the wrong side of the plate (for example, sending a subscription request to a LISTSERV list instead of to the LISTSERV host). Other actions might be considered more inflammatory (for example, cross-posting an irrelevant and offensive message to dozens of random newsgroups).

flame bait An intentionally inflammatory posting designed to elicit a vituperative reaction from various readers and thereby create a flame war.

Hook, Line & Sinker

Sometimes, it's tough to find something good to flame about. Other times, it's just more fun to stir up your very own flame war than join

continues

continued

one that's raging already. Messages obviously aimed at raising the ire (and soliciting flame mail) of a specific group or type of person are known as flame-bait.

While some may claim that only suckers take the bait, others may argue that flaming is a relatively harmless diversion and possibly even a healthy way to vent frustration. Certainly, Bradley Heim sees no problem with a good diatribe now and then, as you can see from his flame-bait below aimed at provoking a lively debate in the `rec.arts.startrek.fandom` newsgroup.

"I just saw a preview screening of the final episode [of Star Trek: The Next Generation], and it was great. When Phyllis Diller started singing 'Somewhere Over the Rainbow' I just cried. Then Picard confessed that he sucks as an actor. Then, Data admitted that he's not a robot, just a person pretending to be a robot.

"In a fond farewell, Troi admitted that she has a crush on Ensign Wesley. As if that weren't enough, Rip Taylor had a guest appearance!!!! I LOVE STARTREK!!!!!! I suggest you videotape this one, because this is going to be one to show the grandkids.

"Cheers!"

"Brad 'Mr.Star Trek' Heim"

∎ ∎ ∎ ∎ ∎ ∎ ∎ ∎ ∎ ∎

flame war A long-running and wide-reaching series of postings or letters detailing an intense hatred of another's point of view, or perhaps just of another individual. Flame wars of particular nastiness are also known as "holy wars" or "jihads."

∎ ∎ ∎ ∎ ∎ ∎ ∎ ∎ **TIP** ∎ ∎ ∎ ∎ ∎ ∎ ∎

flow control A pause in data transmission. When information is rolling by too quickly on your screen, you can usually send a Control-S to bring the data flow to a halt. Pressing Control-Q resumes the transmission.

∎ ∎ ∎ ∎ ∎ ∎ ∎ ∎ ∎ ∎ ∎ ∎ ∎ ∎ ∎ ∎ ∎ ∎ ∎

FNC *See* **Federal Networking Council**.

folder An email application feature that enables you to store messages in defined categories and organize accumulating messages.

followup or **follow-on** A reply to a previous posting to a Usenet newsgroup.

forwarding An email application feature that enables you to send a message that you received to another user.

FQDN *See* **Fully Qualified Domain Name**.

fragmentation The process of breaking an IP packet into smaller pieces to meet the packet-size requirements of a network. The fragments are then reassembled by the IP layer at the destination host. A piece of a packet. *See also* reassembly.

frame A block of data with additional information about the frame number, block size, error-checking codes, and start/stop codes, contained in a header and trailer. A frame is part of the data link layer of the OSI Reference model.

frame relay A standard for ensuring data delivery and integrity for packet-switching networks. Frame relay is a stripped-down version of X.25 and has become the dominant standard in recent years. It may eventually be superseded by cell-switching.

fred A user-friendly interface to X.500.

■■■■■■■■ **TIP** ■■■■■■■■

Free Software Foundation (FSF)
A group devoted to creating and disseminating free software. Founded by Richard Stallman, recipient of a MacArthur "genius" grant, FSF is developing GNU, a set of UNIX-like applications and utilities. You can reach them via anonymous FTP at:
`prep.ai.mit.edu`.

■■■■■■■■■■■■■■■■■■■■

Games People Play

While it's obvious there's a great deal of serious research, scholarship, commerce, diplomacy, and pure science conducted on the Net, there's plenty of goofing off taking place as well.

An entire book could be written (and probably soon will be) about games you can download from and play on the Internet. Rather than list scores of games that won't mean much to the uninitiated, it may prove more helpful to focus on a couple of the most popular games on Net.

Both Bolo and Illuminati are wildly popular games that have developed a cult-like following extending far beyond hard-core netizens.

Bolo is an action/strategy game that can accommodate up to 16 players over a network. Available only for the Macintosh, Bolo offers great graphics and strategies that seem simple at first, but become more complex as the game (and the players' skills) progresses. Bolo is

continues

continued

a genuine obsession among many net-dwellers, and there are scores of files on the Net devoted to the details of the game.

Illuminati is a strategy/role-playing game that is at the same time hilarious and frightening. While at first glance Illuminati seems to be a humorous send-up of conspiracy theories in which you pit groups like the Freemasons against other groups like the Science Fiction Fans, a deeper examination of the game reveals a subtext that closely mirrors the darker workings of life, politics, and the world in general. Illuminati is a multi-player game that also boasts a fanatical following, and there is even a board game version for non-netters.

Download the Bolo Frequently Asked Questions (FAQ) file from the /pub/usenet/news.answers/games/bolo-faq/ directory via anonymous FTP at rtfm.mit.edu. Send email to info@io.com for more information on Illuminati. Consult any of the dozens of games newsgroups under the rec.games listing for more information on all kinds of games.

■ ■ ■ ■ ■ ■ ■ ■ ■ ■

free-WAIS A non-commercial version of the WAIS server distributed by the Clearinghouse for Networked Information Discovery and Retrieval (CNIDR).

freenet Community-based bulletin board systems supported by the National Public Telecommunications Network (NPTN). Like small towns on the electronic superhighway, freenets provide email, discussion groups, local information, and sometimes, connection to the Internet. Although you can visit one of them through gopher or telnet, as an out-of-towner, you may be charged a registration fee.

freeware Software that you can use and distribute without charge. The author still owns the copyright, unless there's a notice to the contrary. *See also* copyright.

frequency A unit of measure that shows how many times per second an electrical signal cycles from maximum to minimum voltage.

fringeware Marginally acceptable software that is made available to the public for free, but one suspects it can't be given away. Also sometimes refers to tasteless shareware meant to annoy or offend; the implication being that only those on the "fringe" would actually hang on to such software.

FTP *See* **File Transfer Protocol**.

Frontier Macintosh software that provides a scripting language and programming environment using Apple events—Apple's inter-application communication protocol. Frontier is a product of UserLand Software.

FSF *See* **Free Software Foundation**.

FTPmail or **FTP by email** A service that provides FTP capability to users who have only email access to the Internet (such as those on CompuServe). You enter an FTP command in the body of the email and send it to an FTPmail server. The server executes the command and sends the result back to you.

full duplex Two-way transmission in which both parties send and receive simultaneously. Some computers can communicate this way. People, despite what they say, cannot. *Contrast* half duplex, and simplex.

full-screen editor *See* **editor**.

Fully Qualified Domain Name (FQDN) The domain name in its entirety that uniquely identifies a specific computer on the Internet. An abbreviation may serve for local addressing purposes, but when sending communications to remote sites, it is necessary to give the full name. For example, the students can exchange mail within the physics department by referring to a computer named "orion," but someone outside of the university must place a FQDN in the Recipient field, such as: "orion.oac.uci.edu." *See also* Domain Name Service, and domain name.

FWIW For What It's Worth. A common shorthand abbreviation seen in chat sessions and email messages.

FYI For Your Information. A common shorthand abbreviation seen in chat sessions and email messages. Also, Internet documents that describe aspects of the Internet, but do not define standards. *Contrast* RFC.

G Standard abbreviation for gigabyte, or one billion bytes.

g,d&r Grinning, ducking, and running. A common shorthand abbreviation seen in chat sessions and email messages, usually after someone makes a sarcastic or mildly inflammatory comment meant primarily in jest.

gated A version of the Routing Information Protocol that is packaged with software available from Cornell University. Use anonymous FTP to: `gated.cornell.edu`.

gateway 1) Software that enables communication between two networks that operate on different protocols. Gateways are written for specific purposes, for example, to provide a link between an Ethernet LAN and an IBM mainframe application that uses SNA (Systems Network Architecture). There is a gateway between BITNET and the Internet.

2) A computer system that enables two dissimilar applications to exchange data, for example, two mail systems with different message formats.

3) Hardware that specifically enables communication between one system and another, such as an IBM 3174 controller gateway.

4) In the original TCP/IP specifications, another name for a router, that is, something that connects networks using dissimilar protocols. Router is considered the more up-to-date term for this function.

GIF *See* **Graphics Interchange Format**.

gif File extension for a picture in graphic interchange format.

gigabyte (G) One billion bytes. Or more precisely, 1,073,741,824 bytes. A giga is 2^{30}.

glitches Intermittent brief failures of undetermined cause. Usually applied to hardware, rather than software, problems.

GNU GNU's Not UNIX—a pun within a pun. GNU is a set of applications and utilities that are being developed and distributed free-of-charge by the Free Software Foundation. GNU and its source code is offered as a replacement for UNIX. It is widely used by UNIX programmers.

TIP

Gopher A menu-driven program that helps you locate and retrieve information on the Internet. Gopher runs on a client/server system. You can access Gopher by either running gopher client software on your local computer or telneting to a gopher server. (See table below "Gopher Servers.") There are also special programs, such as TurboGopher for the Macintosh, that provide a graphical interface for using Gopher.

Gopher Servers

Server Address	Login As...
arx.adp.eisc.edu	wiscinfo
cat.ohiolink.edu	gopher
ecosys.drdr.virginia.edu	gopher
gopher.msu.edu	gopher
gopher.netsys.com	enews
gopher.ora.com	gopher
gopher.virginia.edu	gwis
grits.valdosta.peachnet.edu	gopher
infopath.ucsd.edu	infopath
panda.uiowa.edu	gopher
scilibx.ucsc.edu	infoslug
sunsite.unc.edu	gopher
twosocks.ces.ncsu.edu	gopher
uxi.cso.uiuc.edu	gopher
wsuaix.cis.wsu.edu	wsuinfo

Either way, once you access a Gopher server, you are presented with a menu. From this menu, you can select an item that will take you to another menu—one that probably originates on another computer on another network miles away (although the connection will be transparent to you). This is referred to as "tunneling through Gopherspace."

Gopher Menu Notations

Notation	Means that this entry ...
/	leads to another gopher menu
.	can be read as a text document
<?>	leads to an index
<picture>	can be displayed as a picture if your client software has the capability
<bin>	is a binary file
<tel>	leads to a telnet server
<)	is a sound file
<cso>	leads to a telephone/address program

From a menu, you also can select an item that will automatically FTP a file to you or telnet you to another computer. You can view files and have them mailed to you electronically as well. (See table below, "Gopher Commands.")

Gopher Commands

Command	Description
/	Searches menu for a specified string
0-9	Goes to a specific line
<, -, PgUp, b	Displays previous page
=	Displays description of current item
>, +, PgDn, Space	Displays next page
a	Adds current item to list of bookmarks
D	Downloads a file
d	Deletes bookmark
Down	Moves to the next line
Left or u	Closes current item
m	Returns to the main menu
n	Finds next search item
O	Changes options

continues

Gopher Commands	
q	Quits Gopher
Right or Enter	Displays current item
s	Saves current item
Up	Moves to the previous line
v	Displays list of bookmarks

Developed at the University of Minnesota, Gopher is particularly helpful because it integrates Internet tools such as Telnet , FTP, WAIS, and email. Why is it called "gopher"? Well, the Golden Gopher is the mascot of UM. And like its furry namesake, the program tunnels through the Internet and goes for ("go-fors") your data.

Gopher menus vary significantly from server to server. However, most menus have notations that show what type of item it is. See previous table, "Gopher Menu Notations."

You can also customize Gopher by creating your own menus with bookmarks. *See also* bookmark.

Gopher Book for Windows
Windows Gopher client software. Available by anonymous FTP at: `sunsite.unc.edu`. Using Gopher for Windows, users can explore Gopherspace using a more graphical interface than the standard menu-driven Gopher interface.

Gopher for Nextstep Nextstep Gopher client software. Available by anonymous FTP at: `sonata.cc.purdue.edu`. Using Gopher for Nextstep, users can explore Gopherspace using a more graphical interface than the standard menu-driven Gopher interface.

Gopher+ An upgraded Gopher in development. Among other enhancements, Gopher+ will be able to tell you the size of a file before you download it.

Gopherspace Similar to cyberspace, Gopherspace is the sum of all the menus on all the Gopher servers all over the world. Wow!

GOSIP *See* **Government OSI Profile**.

gov The domain that includes agencies of government, for instance nasa.gov. *See also* domain.

Government OSI Profile (GOSIP)
A set of OSI standards that is used in the procurement of computers by the U.S. Government. The intent is to make sure that any equipment purchased can interoperate with existing systems.

Graphical User Interface (GUI) A command structure with a graphical "front-end" that allows users to manipulate images on their screens to work with data rather than typing commands. Pronounced "gooey." Macintosh, Windows, and NeXT computers sport graphical interfaces. The Xerox Star was one of the first computers with a GUI and inspired much of what was to become the Macintosh operating system. With a SLIP or PPP connection (or faster) to the Internet, you can use software that provides a graphical interface to many of the command-driven tasks of navigating the Internet.

Graphics Interchange Format (GIF) A bit-map graphic file format developed by CompuServe. GIF improves the transport of highly compressed information over networks.

groupware Software that supports collective activities such as scheduling meetings, co-authoring reports, running bulletin board systems, and decision-making processes.

GUI *See* **Graphical User Interface**.

gz File extension for a gzip compression program file.

gzip A file compression program developed by GNU based on UNIX ZIP.

hacker Someone whose seat-of-the-pants programming skills can lead to the back alleys of the electronic highway. The term can be one of endearment or derision, depending on how you want to spin it. In the popular mind, a hacker is a brilliant, but mischievous, school kid like the one in *War Games*. To guardians of the Internet, hackers aren't considered so cute. *Contrast* cracker.

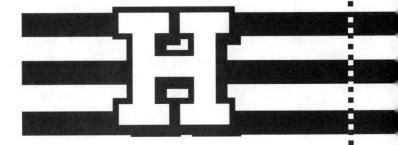

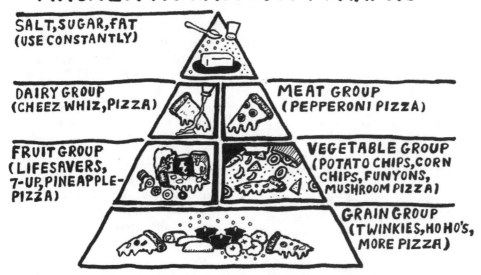

A Jolt to the Hacker Diet

Spending hours—sometimes days—at a stretch jacked into cyberspace tends to spell disaster for a hacker's eating habits. Who has time to cook when there are far-flung corners of the world's largest computer network to be explored?

But oddly enough, bad nutrition seems to be a sort of rite of passage for the hardcore hacker. Who's ever heard of a fanatic computer jock who eats a balanced diet of fruits, vegetables, and poly-unsaturated fats?

continues

continued

It's perhaps a cliche to say that hackers survive mainly on pizza and twinkies, but like so many cliches, this one has its origins in truth. For some crack programmers, the four food groups consist of pizza, sugar, Chinese take-out, and Jolt Cola.

In fact, Jolt Cola (a high-powered soft drink whose motto is "All the sugar and twice the caffeine") is such a staple of the hacker diet, it's a regular topic of discussion on the Net. The `alt.folklore.computer` newsgroup was abuzz for a number of days with rumors about a ban on Jolt in New Zealand and parts of Australia. As it turns out, no one could confirm an outright ban, but there were plenty of shortages spotted.

Still, it never hurts to stock up....

half bridge A device that connects a network to a communications link, such as telephone lines or dedicated circuits such as a PBX. Computers on a network connect to the half bridge via a modem and a communications link. Through the half bridge, computers on one network can communicate with computers on another bridge. Half bridges do not handle addressing information; therefore, messages are transported through the half bridge to the network server, not to a specific workstation. Network software then routes the message to the correct destination. In theory, two half bridges connected to two modems by telephone lines constitutes a full bridge.

half duplex Two-way transmission in which only one end can communicate at a time. After sending data, the sender must wait for an acknowledgment from the receiver before sending more data. The sender and receiver communicate sequentially: In polite conversation, you speak, then I speak. Talk shows such as "Point-Counterpoint" in which two pundits shout at the same time, are not half duplex. *Compare* simplex, and full duplex.

half router A device that is similar to a half bridge with additional functionality. The half router maintains addressing information about both networks so that it can route messages to the intended destination.

handle The nickname you assign yourself when conversing in discussion groups. More prosaically known as a "user name" or "alias." A term picked up from Citizen Band radio (remember "smokey" and "ten four"?) that was populated by critters such as Rubber Duck, Eager Beaver, Fat Man, Net Junkie, CyberWonk and ShadowGal.

handshaking A natural part of the telecommunications etiquette. Refers to the signals sent from a device (such as a printer) to a computer when it (the device) is ready to receive data. Handshaking prevents overloading the device's buffer.

They Walk Among Us

The net is so teeming with "alternative" voices that it sometimes seems as if the "mainstream" is a minority among the rants and raves posted online. If your views tend to follow the straight and narrow path, you're in for an education in the bizarre and eccentric when you begin spelunking the Internet.

In the `alt.alien.visitors` newsgroup, it's not at all uncommon to read postings like John Winston's inside information on, appropriately enough, alien visitors to this planet.

"At the present time and for some time in the past there have been three civilizations of space people coming to the atmosphere of the Earth around our North Pole," Winston writes. He explains further that the UFOs receive clearance from air traffic controllers while hovering in the California desert. "Our people then clear out any planes that are in the area and direct the space people to fly at a certain speed and altitude over the Nevada border to Groom Lake. There they land at night and go into large hangers that are inside the Groom Mountains."

"These space people work with our scientists," Winston continues. "One of the groups of space people are from Zeta Recticuli and I'm not sure where the other ones are from. That is all for now."

While many criticized Winston's posting as pure fantasy and derided him for lack of evidence to support his claim, there is a secret Air Force base at Groom Lake in the Nevada desert that is guarded zealously by mysterious, black-clad goons.

But the real confirmation of Winston's claims came in May, 1994 when the *Weekly World News* reported that a dozen U.S. senators were actually space aliens. Not a single senator denied the allegations, and several finally publicly admitted their dark secret.

continues

continued

In response to the article, Texas Senator Phil Gramm admitted that, while he was born in the U.S., his parents were from the planet Remulak. Christopher Dodd of Connecticut said through his spokesman Marvin Fast that he was relieved "that this is all public," while Bob Maynes, speaking for Arizona's Dennis DeConcini, said that the Senator was "quite distressed" that his "cover has been blown."

■■■■■■■■■■

handshaking line Control circuits in a DTE that manage the flow of data between a computer and a host.

hardware address The unique physical address assigned to a device. For example, a network interface card (NIC) usually has a hardware address written in its memory.

HDLC *See* **High-Level Data Link Control**.

header 1) In an email message, the header is the information above the message that details a message's recipient, sender, subject and origination date, and the time.

2) In a packet, the header precedes the data and contains the source and destination addresses, and error-checking identifiers.

The Blind Leading the Blind

If you think figuring out how to export data from a spreadsheet or spell-check a word processor file can be complicated, don't even think about setting up your own Internet connection.

While there are a few shining examples of excellent tech support on the Net, far too many of the commercial service providers are much more concerned with selling days of access time to huge accounts. There's usually not a lot of time spent helping a confused individual paying $25 per month set up a SLIP account.

Some longtime netizens find a dark humor in this Darwinian world of natural online selection where only the persistent persevere. They've saddled those beleagured tech support staffers (stuck with the task of helping Mac users set their subnet mask settings in MacTCP or other impossible horrors) with the politically incorrect name of "Helper Kellers."

The joke seems to be that many first-time Internet users are dismayed to discover that they know nearly as much about establishing Internet access as do their tech support assistants. The result being help desk calls that sound more like a game of "Wheel of Misfortune" than a systematic attempt to solve software glitches or hardware snafus.

■■■■■■■■■■

heterogeneous network A network that runs more than one kind of network layer protocol.

hexadecimal A system of showing numbers in base16. The numbers "0" through "9" are represented in the usual way, but numbers "10" through "15" have the values "A" through "E". Decimal "10" there-fore, is hexadecimal (or hex) "0A," decimal "20" is hex "14." Hexa-decimal is more quickly processed into binary numbers by computers and therefore a substantial amount of computer code is written in (or converted to) hex.

HGopher for Windows Windows Gopher client software. Available by anonymous FTP at: `lister.cc.ic.ac.uk`.

hierarchical file system A system of storing files in a linear, branched or nested arrangement with subdirectories within a root direc-tory.

hierarchical name A more techni-cally accurate term for domain name.

hierarchical routing A method of dividing a large network into levels to simplify routing and distribute responsibility for administration and maintenance. The Internet has three categories of networks: backbone networks, mid-level networks, and stub networks. Routers on the backbones maintain sufficient information to direct traffic to the mid-level networks, which have information to connect to the stub networks, which have information about local sites.

High Performance Parallel Interface (HPPI) An ANSI standard for connecting supercomputers to other devices, such as routers, frame buffers and other computers. HPPI has a short-distance speed of 800 to 1600 Mbps.

High-Cap *See* **T1**.

High-Level Data Link Control (HDLC) An ISO protocol used in both X.25 and OSI networks that describes the data link layer.

High-Performance Computing Act A federal law sponsored by Vice-President Al Gore when he was in the Senate and signed into law by President Bush in 1991. And everyone thought Bush didn't support technology just because he was shocked to learn that supermarkets had barcode readers.

hit A match to the criterion you specify in a database search. Sometimes a search returns pages and pages of "hits," sometimes nothing at all. When you find exactly what you are looking for, you can utter one of those all-purpose Shakespearean quotes: "A hit, a very palpable hit."

hop The trip a packet takes between one router and the next one on its way to its final destination. Like a person crossing a stream by jumping from rock to rock, a packet "hops" from router to router.

hop count The distance between source and destination in a network as measured by the number of routers a packet passes through.

host A computer that is used by more than one user. Usually, "host" refers to a large computer such as a mainframe that has files, databases, and programs. Hosts can handle an enormous volume of data and run multiple sessions at the same time. Most users access the Internet through a host. A host is said to be either local (the computer you're connected to directly or through dial up) or remote (the computer you're accessing secondarily through the local host, such as when you contact an Archie server or find a file via Gopher). A host is usually distinguished from a server by sheer size. Both an IBM 360 (a mainframe) and an IBM PS/2 can perform the role of server, but the PS/2 (or any personal computer) cannot perform the role of host. *See also* terminal/host computing.

host address *See* **IP address**.

host name The left-most part of the fully-qualified domain name that identifies a specific computer. For example, in `orion.oac.uci.edu`, "orion" is the host name. The rest of the expression is the domain name.

host number *See* **IP address**.

HPCA *See* **High-Performance Computing Act**.

HPCC *See* **High Performance Computing and Communications**.

HPPI *See* **High Performance Parallel Interface**.

HQX File extension for a BinHex file.

HTML *See* **HyperText Markup Language**.

HTTP *See* **HyperText Transport Protocol**.

hub A device that serves as the central connecting point in a star network or cabling system. Hubs are used in an ARCnet LAN to connect computers. They are also used in a message handling service to enable messages to be transferred across a network. *See also* star topology.

HyperCard The Macintosh implementation of hypermedia. Developed by Bill Atkinson while at Apple, HyperCard was hailed by many as the future of multimedia and made significant inroads into certain niches such as the education market. HyperCard is no longer free with every new Macintosh (only a player version is) and is meeting stiff competition from other entry-level scripting/ programming environments.

hypermedia HyperText that is not limited to the written word. Hypermedia can contain graphics, video, and sound—in addition to text. The term was coined by Ted Nelson.

HyperText Markup Language (HTML) The tool used to create linked text files for investigation by World Wide Web browsers.

HyperText Transport Protocol (HTTP) The protocol used by the World Wide Web.

hypertext Writing that is not limited to a linear, one-dimensional plane. A hypertext document contains links to other documents and thus can be read in many dimensions. The term was coined by Ted Nelson in 1965.

HyperWais Macintosh HyperCard WAIS client software. Available by anonymous FTP at: `sunsite.oit.unc.edu`.

HYTELNET HyperTelnet. A database of Telnet sites and other Internet resources that can link to library catalogs, Campus Wide Information Systems, Gopher servers, Bulletin Board Systems (BBSs), database servers, and Wide Area Information Servers (WAIS). Developed at the University of Saskatchewan, HYTELNET automates connection and lookup.

hunter-gatherer Any one of the countless intrepid late-twentieth century homo sapiens in search of data to feed hungry computers.

TIP

Hytelnet for DOS A PC version of Hytelnet. Available by anonymous FTP at: `access.usask.ca`.

Hz Hertz, a measurement of frequency equal to one cycle per second. Named after Heinrich R. Hertz.

I-D *See* **Internet-Draft**.

IAB *See* **Internet Architecture Board**.

IANA *See* **Internet Assigned Numbers Authority**.

IANAL I am not a lawyer. Or it's variant, IANAD, I am not a doctor. A common shorthand abbreviation seen in chat sessions and email messages.

ICMP *See* **Internet Control Message Protocol**.

IEEE *See* **Institute of Electrical and Electronic Engineering**.

IEN *See* **Internet Experiment Note**.

IESG *See* **Internet Engineering Steering Group**.

IETF *See* **Internet Engineering Task Force**.

IGP *See* **Interior Gateway Protocol**.

IINREN *See* **Interagency Interim National Research and Education Network**.

IMAP A recently introduced protocol that defines the storage and retrieval of email. IMAP is similar to the Post Office Protocol (POP).

IMCO In my considered opinion. A common shorthand abbreviation seen in chat sessions and email messages. (A popular variation is IMHO, in my humble opinion.)

immediate commands Certain commands in Delphi that you can type at a prompt and avoid going through a series of menus. This is a useful feature if you're in the middle of a conference, for example, and want to send out a message. Immediate commands are preceded by a "/". Typing "/ send username message," issues a message without taking you out of the conference. Also known as "slash" ("/") commands.

IMO In my opinion. A common shorthand abbreviation seen in chat sessions and email messages.

impedance A medium's (usually a wire or cable of some sort) resistance to an alternating current (AC), measured in ohms. Resistance is the term used when the current is a direct current. *See also* ohm.

IMR *See* **Internet Monthly Report**.

index A file found in an Internet host's directory that describes the directory's contents. It lists files by name with their type, access privileges required, and date. This is usually the first place you check when you're looking for a file. The index may also list other indexes. And so it goes.

■ ■ ■ ■ ■ ■ ■ **TIP** ■ ■ ■ ■ ■ ■ ■

info-server A special address set up on a server to respond automatically to requests for information. For example, you can get of list of anonymous FTP sites by addressing an email to

bitftp@pucc.princeton.edu. Leave the subject field blank and just type the word "ftplist" in the body of the message. In a short time, you will receive a file by email listing the sites.

information hypeway The media-hyped, non-existent fiber-optic network linking such fantastic sites as New York's Museum of Modern Art with places like a grass-hut school-room on a remote island in the South Pacific. While the Internet is far-reaching and widely used, most reporters vastly over-estimate (and hype without restraint) the "super-highway" that net vets argue is still in its "dirt road" days.

information agent Software that searches a variety of databases for information without requiring you to specify a particular location. Archie and Veronica are information agents.

initialization string A string of characters that gets a modem into action, usually "AT" for "attention." *See* Mail Addressing table.

Grumpy Gurus Meet Gabby Greenhorns

When America Online (AOL) launched a gateway providing newsgroup access to it's nearly one million subscribers, the immediate result was a rather staggering wave of new postings to the more than 5,000 USENET newsgroups. While there was the ocassional AOL user who made typical "newbie" breaches of netiquette such as asking obvious questions covered in the Frequently Asked Questions file, most AOL users followed protocols (or simply read news articles without posting responses).

Still, in the great Internet tradition of making megabytes out of bits, scores of veteran netters spent hours posting flames, gripes, and general tirades decrying the AOL invasion. For a while, it seemed that no one would speak out in defense of the AOL greenhorns, until one fellow pointed out that "so far, I have had to wade through about three times the garbage from the self-righteous as from AOL [people]. Would everyone please shut up!"

■ ■ ■ ■ ■ ■ ■ ■ ■ ■

insert mode A state in which anything you type is inserted as text into the document or message you are working on, as opposed to being interpreted as a command to the application you are running. (The latter state is called "command mode.") In a UNIX editor such as vi, you are in command mode by default.

Institute of Electrical and Electronic Engineering (IEEE) A professional organization that has defined a variety of standards. The IEEE (the abbreviation is pronounced I-triple-E) "802" group has developed standards for LAN technologies. *See also* 802.1, 802.2, 802.3, 802.4, and 802.5

Integrated Services Digital Network (ISDN) A circuit-switched digital network that integrates voice and data into a single cable. It also provides an economical connection between LANs. ISDN standards are specified by CCITT. *See also* circuit-switched network.

interactive Systems that respond to instructions that you type at the keyboard. There is a give and take between you, the user, and the system you are interacting with. An interactive session normally involves a system prompt and a user response. *Contrast* with automated programming.

interactive talk A direct, back-and-forth online conversation between two users that takes place in real time. *Contrast* to the store-and-forward technique of email.

See also talk, and Internet Relay Chat.

Interagency Interim National Research and Education Network (IINREN) A networking infrastructure and operating system that is the research and development stage. Eventually IINREN will be part of the National Research and Education Network (NREN).

interest groups *See* **special interest group**.

interface (Noun) Defined set of inputs to a device such as a parallel printer interface that has 25 wires, each one having a defined function. Also the method by which a user interacts or communicates with a local computer or remote host.

(Verb) To interact with a specific device so that data can be exchanged in a defined fashion.

Interior Gateway Protocol (IGP) A protocol that specifies the distribution of routing information among the routers within an autonomous system. In this case, "gateway" refers to the same type of device as "router."

Intermediate System (IS) An OSI system that transports packets across a network in much the same way as an IP router. An IS functions on the Network layer of the OSI Reference Model. *See also* Open Systems Interconnection, and router.

Intermediate System to Intermediate System protocol (IS-IS) A protocol that routes both OSI and IP packets. The OSI IGP.

See also Open Systems Interconnection, and Interior Gateway Protocol.

International Organization for Standardization (ISO) As part of its mission to promote cooperation in science and technology, this international body publishes standards affecting, among other things, computers and communications. Its most notable contribution to networking technology is arguably the OSI Reference Model. ANSI represents the U.S. among the national standards organizations of the 89-member countries.

International Telegraph and Telephone Consultative Committee (CCITT) An international organization made up of telecommunications companies that defines standards—although CCITT diplomatically calls them "recommendations." CCITT is part of a United Nations agency, the International Telecommunications Union (ITU). CCITT holds plenary sessions every four years (most recently in 1992) to consider new standards. *See also* X.25, X.400, and X.500. The initials, CCITT, stand for the French name: Comite Consultatif International de Telegraphique et Telphonique.

Internet (Capitalized) The network of 45,000 interconnected networks in 70 countries that use the TCP/IP networking communications protocol. It is the largest network of computers in the world. The Internet (when preceded by "the" everyone knows what internet you're talking about) provides email, file transfer, news, remote login, and access to thousands of databases. You can play games (*see also* MUD), engage in conversations with people around the world (*see also* Internet Relay Chat), and build your own library of journals, books, and images (*see also* Archie, World-Wide Web, and Gopher). The Internet is made up of three different kinds of networks: high-speed backbone networks such as NSFNET and MILNET, mid-level networks such as universities and corporations, and stub networks such as individual LAN's. It is informally known by other names such as "WorldNet," "the Net," "the web," and the ever-popular "electronic superhighway." *See also* outernet, and Matrix.

internet (Not Capitalized) 1) The result of connecting two or more networks so that computers in each network can share data and devices. The different networks on an internet are connected by routers. An internet does not necessarily use TCP/IP. In an internet, a network is connected to at least one other network. For example, Network A is connected to Network B, which is connected to Network C, and so on. In this way, networks are interconnected, but this doesn't mean all the networks are directly connected to each other. Network A is not necessarily directly connected to Network C.

2) A specific term applied to AppleTalk networks connected by AppleTalk routers. Sometimes referred to as an "internetwork."

Internet address *See* **IP address**.

Internet Architecture Board (IAB) A group that coordinates the development and maintenance of TCP/IP protocols and manages certain aspects of the Internet, such as standards and address allocation. The IAB also oversees the work of the IETF and the IRTE. At one time, the IAB was called the "Internet Activities Board." The IAB meets quarterly. To learn more about the IAB, use anonymous FTP: `ietf.cnri.reston.va.us`.

Internet Assigned Numbers Authority (IANA) The official registry for a range of Internet protocol parameters, including port, protocol and enterprise numbers, terminal and system identifiers. The sanctioned values are listed in the "Assigned Numbers" document (STD2). To request a number assignment, send an email to: `iana@isi.edu`. *See also* assigned numbers, and STD.

Internet Control Message Protocol (ICMP) A necessary addition to the Internet Protocol that specifies the generation of error messages, test packets, and informational messages related to IP. ICMP supports the PING command that is used to determine if a remote system is online.

Internet Engineering Steering Group (IESG) A group that provides an initial technical review of Internet standards and manages the IETF. The Chair of the IETF and Area Directors make up the body of the IESG.

Internet Engineering Task Force (IETF) A group of research volunteers that responds to technical problems and submits reports and proposals to the Internet Architecture Board (IAB). The IETF is made up of computer technicians, network administrators, vendors, and researchers who coordinate the operation, management, and evolution of the Internet. They also assist in disseminating new technologies that originate from the IRTF. The IETF meets three times a year. To learn more about the IETF, use anonymous FTP: `ietf.cnri.reston.va.us`.

Internet Experiment Note (IEN) A series of Internet reports that had been published along with RFCs, but are no longer operative.

TIP

Internet Hunt A monthly quiz that tests your ability to use the resources and services available on the Internet. You are asked 10 questions that you can only answer using the Internet. Use gopher to reach the host `gopher.cic.net`. From there on, you must rely on your own inter-sleuthing skills.

■ ■ ■ ■ ■ ■ ■ ■ # TIP ■ ■ ■ ■ ■ ■ ■ ■

Internet Mailing Guide A list of networks and their various addressing formats, maintained by Ajay Shekhawat at the State University of New York (Buffalo). For example, it shows that to send an email to someone on America Online from Internet you need to use this address format:

username@aol.com. You can access the Guide by anonymous FTP. *See also* address format table.

■ ■ ■ ■ ■ ■ ■ ■ ■ ■ ■ ■ ■ ■ ■ ■ ■ ■ ■ ■

Internet Monthly Report (IMR)
A monthly publication about networking matters that is reported to the Internet Research Group.

Wanna Bet That the Walls Have Ears?

While it's always a great idea to check the Internet for information, tips, and other tidbits about a town or country you're about to visit, the real depth of the Net's information wells becomes apparent when you combine a special interest with a remote destination. Looking for the best beer selection in Hamburg, a hot pick for the horse track in San Diego, or a fun-loving dominatrix in Taipei? Check the Net!

For instance, let's say you're into scanning—that most voyeuristic of hobbies where you can eavesdrop on everything from cellular phone calls to police dispatches using a handheld receiver. You're headed to Las Vegas for the National Shower Curtain Ring Wholesaler's Convention, and other than finding a few tips on how to work the casinos for fun and profit, you'd like to know what frequencies to program into your scanner for maximum surveilance potential.

First, check out the `rec.gambling` newsgroup. If you've got a specific question about a resort, game, or show, there are experts here who can give you a straight answer. But if you want the proverbial jackpot of gambler's inside info, download the `rec.gambling` Frequently Asked Questions (FAQ) file. It's a veritable mother lode— crammed with tidbits on everything from counting cards to scoring a free ("comp") room. The file is also packed with phone numbers and reservation information for scores of airlines, hotels, and casinos.

If you're still not up on the angles, check out the gambling files archive in the `/pub/rec.gambling/` directory available via anonymous FTP at `soda.berkeley.edu`.

As for the scanner frequencies, you can check with the contributors in the `alt.radio.scanner` newsgroup, where you're likely to find

that the security guards at Caesars Palace broadcast at 451.7 and
456.7 mhz (duplex) while the Las Vegas Metro Police force chats at
158.745 mhz. If you want more info, you can check out the scanner
(and shortwave, ham, and other radio) archives in the `/pub/dx/`
directory via anonymous FTP at `nic.funet.fi`.

TIP

**Internet Network Information
Center (InterNIC)** A service
management system sponsored by
the National Science Foundation,
which includes registration services
provided by Network Solutions,
Inc., directory and database
services provided by AT&T, and
information services provided by
General Atomics/CERFnet. For
more information on the InterNIC,
send email to:
`info@internic.net`.

Scout's Honor

Keeping up with what's new on the Internet could be a full-time job.
In fact, it is. The InterNIC, an organization funded by the National
Science Foundation and dedicated to assisting the research, science,
education, and business communities make better use of the Internet,
employs "info scouts" to keep track of and report on important new
developments on the Net.

Each week, the InterNIC releases "The Scout Report," which summa-
rizes online activities, new resources and other important "Internet
finds." You can access the Scout Report in a number of popular
flavors, including via email, Gopher, and Word-Wide Web. (The
Gopher and Web versions contain active links to resources mentioned in the report.)

continues

continued

A Scout report from a week in May, 1994 included information about, among other things: The U.S. Food & Drug Administration World Wide Web Server, the *Journal of Artificial Intelligence Research*, the Open Government Pilot (providing access to various segments of the Canadian federal government), Window-to-Russia (a project providing access to a variety of information resources from and about Russia), NetResults (a network of people and teams working to reinvent government), and a bi-monthly newsletter for people with hand, arm, or shoulder injuries caused by computer work.

To receive the electronic mail version of the "Scout Report" each Friday, you can join the scout-report mailing list by sending mail to: `majordomo@is.internic.net` with the words "subscribe scout-report" in the body of the message. World-Wide Web users can get the report from `http://www.internic.net/` while Gopher users can retrieve it from the information services directory at `is.internic.net`. For details, contact `scout@internic.net`.

■■■■■■■■■■

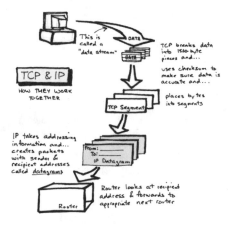

Internet Protocol (IP) The protocol that routes data between hosts on the Internet. The IP is the essence of the Internet: theoretically, it could function without the other protocols, but they could not function without the IP. The IP is connectionless because it routes each datagram separately. It is also considered a best effort protocol because it does not guarantee delivery; simply that it will try its best. This means that a datagram may be damaged in transit, or thrown away by a busy router, or simply never make it to its destination. The resolution of these problems is the work of the Transmission Control Protocol (TCP). IP's mission is to get the data across the Internet to its destination. It also provides a great degree of flexibility—nodes and even whole networks can be added on without bringing down the rest of the network.

Where Did the Internet Protocol Come From?

The IP was developed to meet strict requirements established by the U.S. Department of Defense. The DoD, with its far-flung and complex operations, was contending with the same dilemmas that were besetting large corporations. The juggernaut of DoD installations had a multitude of large computers built by different manufacturers. There were a variety of networks in place and they seemed to be expanding every day. There was a mix of new technologies and old technologies. There was an increasing demand to expand and up-grade services, and especially, to interconnect existing systems. The DoD needed to get its computers to work together in both a connectionless and connection-oriented mode. The designers of the IP selected a connectionless network layer architecture (correspond-ing to the network layer of the OSI Reference model) as best meeting the DoD's requirements.

TIP

Internet Relay Chat (IRC) A global CB-like dialog that involves people sending messages to each other in real time. This is an expansion of the UNIX talk pro-gram developed in Finland. While talk allows two users to converse, IRC enables many people to engage in the conversation. (Many IRC users are college students wasting time as only they seem to be able to, but educators and businesspeople use IRC as a sort of "Internet conference call" because it is cheaper than dialing long distance and the chats can be logged and saved, providing a word-for-word record of the conversation.) There are currently hundreds of conversation groups or channels taking place. IRC is actually a network of servers, each taking requests from individual client programs. *Compare* interac-tive talk.

Is That a Terminal I See Before Me?

Internet Relay Chat (IRC) is a feature on the Net that enables users at any terminal hooked into the Internet to type comments back and forth in real time. While the Internet Relay Chat service is used by folks around the world to discuss everything from the weak electro-magnetic force to the number of licks it takes to get to the center of a Tootsie Pop, it's also sometimes used for projects that just couldn't be pulled off any other way.

continues

continued

Like a global Shakespearean theater, for instance. On April 23, 1994 (which would have been Shakespeare's 430th birthday if he hadn't shuffled off his mortal coil), a group of Internet Relay Chatters performed Macbeth, or something that seemed vaguely familiar to Macbeth, only updated for the digital age.

In an adaptation the *Los Angeles Times* labeled "more Billy Idol than Billy Shakespeare," performers from such far flung sites as Israel and South Africa delivered lines like:

LadyM: "Did you do it? Idiot! You were supposed to leave the daggers on the guards. Give them to me, and for God's sake, go clean up."

PCbeth: "I'll never get to sleep after this. Where's the Prozac?"

While the typical audience for an online Shakespeare performance is relatively small (about 100 folks), producer Stuart Harris is determined to continue organizing such performances. After a thunderstorm cut short his debut performance of Hamlet ("Hamnet"), Harris repeated the drama two months later. He's now planning an adaptation of a Tennesee Williams play that will debut on the net as "An IRC Channel Named Desire."

■ ■ ■ ■ ■ ■ ■ ■ ■ ■

Internet Research Steering Group (IRSG) The group that oversees the IRTF.

Internet Research Task Force (IRTF) An IAB group that investigates long-term Internet issues ranging from the impact of tens of millions of Americans receiving interactive cable in their homes to what new technologies are needed to cope with the projected growth of the Internet. Some of the advances they have supported are multi-cast audio/video conferencing and privacy enhanced mail.

Internet Society (ISOC) A nonprofit organization that supports the development of networking technology and promotes the use of the Internet in scientific and academic communities. ISOC publishes *The Internet Society News* quarterly and produces the INET conference annually.

Internet-Draft (I-D) Works-in-progress. The Internet Engineering Task Force (IETF) writes draft documents about issues such as network problems and new technologies. I-D's are circulated through various working groups for a six-month period for review. After that time, they are likely to be revised or superseded by other documents.

TIP

Internetiquette Rules of the road for netfarers. Even if you can't see your fellow citizens of the electronic highways, it's still a good idea to mind your manners. Some of the more commonly preached guidelines: Make sure the address is correct. Don't be vulgar. Don't add another link to a chain letter. Don't SHOUT (send messages in ALL UPPERCASE LETTERS). Don't flame (get abusive)—cool off before you send your anger out into the ether. Also called "netiquette."

Internetwork Packet Exchange (IPX) Novell's NetWare network-layer protocol that specifies addressing, routing, and switching packets. Routers with IPX enable clients and servers to communicate across interconnected LANs.

internetwork An AppleTalk network.

InterNIC *See* **Internet Network Information Center**.

InterNIC Registration Service One of the three services offered by the InterNIC. The registration service provides information about Internet Domains, networks, and machines. *See also* yellow pages, and InterNIC.

interoperability The capacity of devices made by different manufacturers, running different operat-ing systems, or using different protocols, to interact together and exchange information across a network.

interrupts Control-key commands such as CTRL-C and CTRL-Z that abort, stop, or pause an ongoing activity.

TIP

InterSLIP Macintosh Serial Line Interface Protocol (SLIP) software. When combined with MacTCP, you can connect directly to the Internet. Developed by InterCon Systems Corporation and available as freeware by anonymous FTP at: `ftp.intercon.com`.

IP *See* **Internet Protocol**.

IP address The Internet Protocol address uniquely identifies each machine on the Internet. It is made up of 4 sets of numbers separated by periods or "dots," hence it is sometimes called "dot addressing." Technically, it is a 32-bit (4 octet) binary value. For example: 123.453.112.12. This is the addressing scheme usually only known to computers and network honchos. Most users only know (and care to know) the familiar English-language host name provided by the DNS (such as `angelo@plexcore.com`). The largest number that can appear in an IP address is 255.

IPX *See* **Internetwork Packet Exchange**.

IR *See* **internet router**.

IRC *See* **Internet Relay Chat**.

Ircle Macintosh Internet Relay Chat (IRC) client software. Available by anonymous FTP at: mac.archive.umich.edu.

IRSG *See* **Internet Research Steering Group**.

IRTF *See* **Internet Research Task Force**.

IS *See* **Intermediate System**.

IS-IS *See* **Intermediate System to Intermediate System**.

ISDN *See* **Integrated Services Digital Network**.

ISO *See* **International Organization for Standardization**.

ISO Development Environment (ISODE) Software that enables systems using the Open System Interconnection to interact with a TCP/IP networks.

ISOC *See* **Internet Society**.

ISODE *See* **ISO Development Environment**.

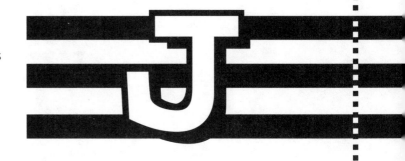

jabber To transmit meaningless data. A faulty condition that sometimes occurs in both networks and the humans that use them.

jell-o-**vision** Term used to describe the poor quality of video displayed on most PCs when using a standard such as QuickTime or participating in an Internet videoconference. Because of limitations in data throughput, many Internet videoconferences appear as if they're being viewed through a thin, wiggling piece of Jell-o.

joe A UNIX editor.

Joint Photographic Experts Group (JPEG) A committee working under the International Standards Organization (ISO) that has proposed a universal standard for the compression and decompression of still images. Pronounced "jay-peg."

JPEG *See* Joint Photographic Experts Group.

jpeg File extension for JPEG-compressed images.

JVNCnet A Northeastern U.S. and worldwide Internet provider. For information, send email to: `market@jvnc.net`.

K, KB, Kbyte *See* **Kilobyte**.

KA9Q A version of TCP/IP for amateur packet radio systems.

Kbps Kilobits (one thousand bits) per second. *See also* bits per second.

Kerberos A security system developed at MIT that uses encryption to prevent anyone from unlocking computer passwords and breaking into files and directories.

Kermit A terminal emulation program and file transfer protocol developed at Columbia University. Kermit is the slowest file transfer protocol, but it is useful when sending 7-bit characters. (Naturally, despite its lackluster transfer speed—or perhaps because of it—Kermit is a favorite of many educational institutions. Its status as freeware has also endeared it to thrifty educators everywhere.) Yes, it's named in honor of Sesame Street's Kermit the Frog.

kill A news reader feature that enables you to specify criteria so that certain articles are automatically excluded from display. This way you can screen out articles by author or subject. *Contrast* auto select.

Kilobyte (K, KB, Kbyte) 1,024 (or 2^{10}) bytes. Commonly used to measure a computer's memory (for example, 8,000K) or a floppy disk's capacity (800K). In addition, there are many inexact approximations represented by a kilobyte: approximately one thousand characters, 205 five-letter words, or a screen of text.

KIS *See* **Knowbot Information Services**.

Knowbot Information Services (KIS) A service that automates the procedures used to find a name or address. KIS is not a database, but a program that searches other databases for information. Still in a limited experimental stage, KIS can take a single query and access other servers running whois, X.500, and finger. It also can access MCIMail and RIPE.

Knowbots Used informally to mean "robotic librarians," knowbots are programs that search for information. Actually, the term is a registered trademark of the Corporation for National Research Initiatives.

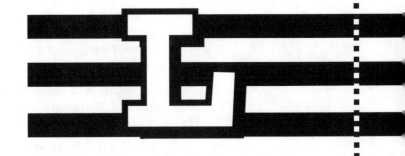

LAN *See* **Local Area Network**.

LAN adapter *See also* network interface card, controller.

LAP *See* **Link Access Protocol**.

LAT *See* **Local Area Transport**.

layer *See* **protocol layers**.

leaf site A computer of the Usenet network that communicates with only one other machine, rather than distributing news to other sites.

leased line A permanent private telephone line that is leased from the phone company, usually to connect a local network to a WAN or an Internet service provider. *See also* dedicated line.

Library of Congress Nextstep software that enables you to search through the Library of Congress catalog and purchase books via a mail application that comes with it. Available by anonymous FTP at: `sonata.cc.purdue.edu`.

Geek Like Me

Longtime netdwellers can attest that spending too much time on the Internet can be detrimental to your social life (although your virtual social life will be in great shape). People may start to wonder why you spend so much time at your computer. They'll whisper about you behind your back. They'll even start to call you a geek!

But is that so bad? The Internet is brimming with geeks living fulfilling, productive lives. Take Gary Watson, for instance. Gary posted a stirring "confession" to the `alt.geeks newsgroup` (where else?!), and it's excerpted here for the benefit of the geek in all of us struggling to get out.

"Hello...my name is Gary, and I'm a geek."

[Hi Gary!]

"I drive a Saturn Station wagon and I think it is a cool car. Last week I made an appointment to take the car in for its 30k service. When I got to the dealer's this morning, my odometer read 29,993, so I drove

continues

continued

3.5 miles past the dealer's and made a U-turn so as to arrive with 30k even."

"When I go on vacation, I have each town listed on a notepad with the ETA. I allow for 15-minute rest stops every 150 miles and 30 minutes for meals. My wife hates this."

"When I drink milk, I think about how funny it would be if I cracked up and sprayed the milk out my nose. This is a self-fulfilling prophecy."

Gary Watson
Los Gatos, CA

■ ■ ■ ■ ■ ■ ■ ■ ■ ■

line length A setting some online services use to change the number of lines that are displayed on your screen. Some people say "line width," but they are thinking in terms of the width of the screen, not the length of the line or characters. Normally, line length is set to 80.

line width A setting some online services use to change the number of characters that are displayed across your screen.

line-oriented interface A display that only shows one line at a time. *Contrast* screen-oriented. *See also* character-based interface.

linefeed A command or control character that advances the cursor or printer paper one line. A linefeed is an end-of-line terminator. The line feed control character is ASCII 10. In the text files typically exchanged across the Internet, the line feed character sometimes presents problems. With a word processor, there is no need to advance a line when you are typing because it will automatically word wrap based on the right margin setting. However, some mail editors are more rudimentary and require you to force a line feed by pressing the Return (or Enter) key after typing a line of text. So when you download a text file, for example a mail message, and open it with an word processor, you may find that every line has a carriage return. Some word processors let you open a document in text (which has carriage returns) or text with layout (which forces a word wrap on the incoming text). There are also shareware programs that strip out the extra carriage returns.

Another complication for users exchanging files across networks is that the end-of-line terminator varies from computer to computer.

This means that if you open a DOS text file with a Macintosh software, you will find that each line begins with a rectangle that indicates the line feed placed there by the DOS program.

On the other hand, if you open a Macintosh text file on a PC running DOS, the PC program will not recognize the carriage returns as line feeds and there will be no line breaks at all. Many of the advanced word processors can cope with this and there are also several shareware products which deal with this dilemma as well. *See also* carriage return.

IBM PC	Carriage Return plus Linefeed
Macintosh	Carriage Return
Amiga	Linefeed
UNIX	Linefeed

TIP

Link Access Protocols (LAP)
AppleTalk Data link layer protocols that specify the interface to network hardware. There are several implementatioons of LAP: ALAP (Apple Talk Link Access Protocol), LLAP (Local Talk Link Access Protocol), ELAP (Ethernet Link Access Protocol), TLAP (TokenRing Link Access Protocol) and ARCnet LAP (ARCnet Link Access Protocol).

list (Verb) To display the contents of a flie on your screen or send the file to your printer, depending on the context in which the command is given.

(Noun) A LISTSERV list.

TIP

LISTSERV An automated mailing-list distribution system that started on the BITNET/EARN network. LISTSERV is a program that runs on IBM mainframes and responds to your request to add or delete your name to one of the hundreds of discussion lists currently active. As an Internet user, you subscribe to a LISTSERV mailing list by sending an email to the computer on which LISTSERV is running. You don't have to know the name of the machine that actually distributes the mailings. All computers with the LISTSERV software know the location of all the LISTSERV lists. As a subscriber, you can exchange messages with others on the list by addressing a message to the list. All other subscribers receive your message and any reply to your message is delivered to all subscribers. LISTSERV stands for List Server. LISTSERV is so ungainly—why not simply add the "e" and call it LISTSERVE? The answer is that LISTSERV runs on IBM computers and "List Server" was chopped down to 8 characters.

Do NOT send your subscribe or unsubscribe command to the list itself; make sure it is addressed to LISTSERV. The people on the list can't do anything with your request but give it the boot.

LLAP *See* **LocalTalk Link Access Protocol**.

LLC *See* **Logical Link Control**.

Local Area Network (LAN) A group of computers that are located in one area and are usually connected by less than 1,000 feet of cable. Typically, a LAN might interconnect a number of computers and printers on a single floor or in a single building. LANs can be connected together, but if two or more LAN's are connected by modems and telephone lines, the larger network constitutes what is called a WAN. LANs come in different physical configurations (called "topologies"), the most popular being bus, ring, and star. There are also different sets of protocols and technologies available; the most dominant in the market are Ethernet, Token Ring, and to a lesser extent, ARCnet.

LANs make it possible for computers to share files and peripherals such as printers and servers. Being connected to a LAN also enables computers from different vendors to interoperate—to work together. *See also* Token Ring, Ethernet, ring topology, star topology, and bus topology.

Local Area Transport (LAT) Digital Computer's architecture for connecting terminal servers on Ethernet networks to host computers. LAT is designed to cut down on network traffic by distributing processing from host computers.

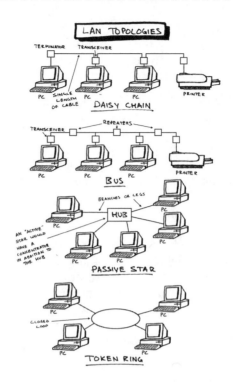

local An adjective that is applied to devices or processes that are under your direct control, as opposed to remote devices that are not under your control. The printer directly attached to your computer's printer port is a local printer. The printer that you connect to via a network is a remote printer.

In networking, local refers to the host on which you have an account. *Contrast* remote.

local echo *See* **echo**.

local node In a network of computers, the system that you access directly. The other computers are remote nodes.

LocalTalk Apple's networking hardware that is a standard feature of the Macintosh computer. The transmission speed (bandwidth) of LocalTalk is 230 Kbps. LocalTalk hardware includes cables, connection boxes, and other equipment for connecting computers and other devices. LocalTalk was formerly called the AppleTalk Personal Network Cabling System. You can make a low-cost LAN network using LocalTalk and twisted-pair wiring. LocalTalk operates at the Physical layer of the protocol architecture.

log in Identifying yourself and making a connection to a computer's operating system. This usually means typing in a valid username and password in response to the computer's prompts. Computers that are accessed by more than one user, (such as online information services,) generally have a log in process. Personal computers do not. Also known as "sign-on" or "logon."

log off Signaling to a computer that you are terminating a session, whether interacting with a host, an online information service, or a BBS. There are various ways of telling a computer or service that you are through for the day. Paul Simon sang about "50 ways to leave your lover." There are almost as many ways to leave your session. Some examples:

hangup	Tymnet
quit	Archie
logout	various UNIX shells
exit	FTP session
bye	telnet

Logical Link Control (LLC)
1) The IEEE 802 standard that specifies the presentation of a uniform user interface so that the user does not need to know what network medium is being used. In other words, as a user, you don't need to know if the cabling is twisted pair or coaxial.

2) A Data Link layer that is defined in IEEE 802.2. LLC specifies the exchange of data between two systems sharing the same medium.

Logical Unit (LU) The software that interacts with the network in IBM SNA networks.

logical Adjective applied to entities that are defined by computers but have no physical existence.

logical byte A byte that is not the usual eight-byte length. Normally a byte is the smallest unit that can be handled by a computer. Some computers, however, use a byte of a different size. *See also* octet.

LOL Laughing Out Loud. A common shorthand abbreviation seen in chat sessions and email messages.

Los Nettos A Los Angeles, CA, Internet provider. For information, send email to: `los-nettos-request@isi.edu`.

Digital Machismo

If the Internet is rich with valuable information and useful news and statistics, it's positively overflowing with pointless bickering and sniping. Not all debates on the Net degenerate to the point of a flame war. Many net-combatants bubble along at a snappy pace, content to argue for the sake of arguing.

Many of the disagreements center around arcane technical information, and newsgroups and mailing lists are flooded with carefully documented arguments about which modem is fastest, which monitor displays the most colors, and which co-processor can perform the most floating-point calculations per nanosecond. Other arguments (such as Mac vs. PC/Windows) are timeless classics that will never be decided in a century of cybersquabbles.

This "digital machismo" seems to be a cherished part of life on the Net, so you'd better get used to it. Where else but on the Internet will you find people not only arguing that there's a distinct difference between a geek and a nerd, but bickering about which is worse?!

continues

continued

Below is a list of 10 actual questions vehemently argued (sometimes for weeks at a time) in the proving grounds of cyberspace. Answers (based on group consensus, editorial liberty, or coin toss) appear at the end of the list.

1. Could the Death Star destroy the Borg ship?

2. Which is better: Nintendo or Sega?

3. Which is bigger: a Slurpee or a Big Gulp?

4. Who's more annoying: Barney or Mr. Rogers?

5. Who'd win in a fight: Fred Flintstone (brawn) or George Jetson (brains)?

6. Which is more "cyberpunkish"?: *Wired* or *Mondo 2000*?

7. Could Jean-Luc Picard defeat James T. Kirk?

8. Which is worse for you: a Twinkie or a Zinger?

9. Who's funnier: Letterman or Leno?

10. Who's more deadly to humans: Alien or Predator?

9. Letterman; 10. tie

1. Borg; 2. Sega; 3. same size; 4. Barney; 5. Jetson; 6. *Mondo 2000*; 7. Kirk; 8. Zinger;

■■■■■■■■■ TIP ■■■■■■■■

Louis Mamakos' SLIP Nextstep software that enables connection to the Internet via the Serial Line Interface Protocol (SLIP). Available by anonymous ftp at `sonata.cc.purdue.edu`.

ls-lr UNIX command. List full information about the current directory and its contents.

LU 6.2 A part of IBM's Advanced Peer-to-Peer Communications (APPC).

lurking Reading the discussions going on in a mailing list without posting any messages yourself. A lurker is a non-contributing subscriber. Sounds worse than it is. When you're new to electronic socializing, it's like being the new kid on the block: you hang around the playground watching the other kids run around. Sooner or later you're bound to overcome your shyness and jump in.

MAC *See* **Media Access Control**.

MAC address The label that identifies a piece of hardware connected to a shared media.

MacPPP Macintosh Point to Point Protocol (SLIP) software. When combined with MacTCP, you can connect directly to the Internet. Developed by Merit Computer Network and available as freeware by anonymous FTP at `merit.edu`.

macro A method of incorporating a string of characters and/or commands into a single keystroke or combination of keystrokes. Terminal emulation programs and keyboard program such as QuicKeys for the Macintosh enable you to create your own macros.

MacSLIP Macintosh Serial Line Interface Protocol (SLIP) or CSLIP (compressed version of SLIP) software. When combined with MacTCP, you can connect directly to the Internet. Developed by Hyde Park Software.

MacTCP Apple Computer's TCP/IP driver. When placed in the System Folder, you can configure a TCP/IP connection including setting IP addresses, gateways, and Domain Name Servers. Available with many commercial packages. For information send email to `apda@applelink.apple.com`.

Mail Exchange Record (MX) A Domain Name System record type that identifies the host that processes mail for domain.

mail or **mail program** Software that enables users to send and receive messages. Most mail programs today have the following set of standard features: replying, aliasing, forwarding, saving (into directories or folders), and conferencing. They also usually have the capability of exchanging mail with other mail programs. Nonstandard features that are increasingly becoming the norm are: carbon copies, blind carbon copies, signature files, notification of receipt, notification of read, message cancelling, and some method of attaching text files. Also called "email programs" or "mailers."

mail address The specific combination of username and computer name that is the destination of an email transmission. Addressing formats vary widely and confusingly from network to network. *See also* table below, "Mail Addressing Formats," which is based on information taken from the "Internet Mailing Guide" maintained by AJay Shekhawat at the State University of New York (Buffalo).

Mail Addressing Formats

Provider	TO Internet from provider	FROM Internet to provider
America Online	username@host	username@aol.com
AppleLink	username@host@IPaddress	username@applelink.apple.com
AT&T Mail	internet!host!username	username@attmail.com
BITNET	username@host@gateway	username%site.bitnet@gateway
CompuServe	>internet:username@host	nnnn.nnnn@compuserve.com
Delphi	in%"username@host"	username@delphi.com
Envoy	[RFC-822=\ "username(a) host\"	att!attmail!mhs!envoy! username@UUNET.UU.NET
Genie	username@host@INET#	username@genie.geis.com
NSI-DECNET	AMES::\"username@host\"	username@host.SPAN.NASA..GOV
THEnet	UTADNX::WINS% "username@host"	username%host.decnet @utadnx.cc.utexas.edu

mail bridge A device that connects networks and screens incoming email. The mail bridge only forwards to the remote network email that meets specific criteria.

mail exploder A program that delivers an email message to all addresses on a mailing list. It's the basic concept of mailing lists and LISTSERV: you send a message to one address (the mail exploder), and it in turn sends out your communication to every name on its recipient list.

mail gateway The point where email from one network is passed to the email system of another, possibly dissimilar, network. If necessary, the mail gateway reformats the message from the sender so that it can be delivered and understood by the receiver.

mail path An address that consists of the machine names that are needed to direct electronic mail from one user to another. A method of addressing email that is used mainly in UUCP networks.

mail reflector A mail address that automatically forwards any mail sent to it to other addresses. This device is used to build discussion groups.

mail server An application that distributes email items in response to requests.

mailbox The directory on a host computer where your email messages are stored. When you log on, the mail program notifies you that you have mail.

Tonya Harding: Electronic Privacy Poster Girl

The Internet and emerging information highway was clearly one of the biggest stories of 1993—perhaps in part because hundreds of journalists discovered (virtually simultaneously) the wonders of email and newsgroups.

Even the most over-hyped story of 1994—the Tonya Harding/Nancy Kerrigan saga—featured an information highway spin when a number of reporters hacked into Tonya Harding's email account during the Winter Olympics in Lillehammer, Norway. (Although Tonya wasn't screaming "Why me?!" after her email had been hacked, she probably wasn't thrilled about the incident.) According to Dave Barry, syndicated columnist for *The Miami Herald*, Harding's password was easily guessed (or lifted) from information on her Olympic Village ID badge.

Once the story broke that Harding's email had been hacked (and apparently featured nothing of interest to a news-starved civilization), journalists who'd violated Harding's privacy for the sake of tabloid headlines generally fell into two camps regarding their feelings about the matter: unrepentant and proud.

Internet citizens responded mainly with a mixture of fear and disgust to the media's lack of respect for the sanctity of electronic mail. But the saga isn't over just yet: a few particularly offended net dwellers have vowed revenge and are openly planning to hack the email accounts of various reporters, posting the fascinating mail of journalism's brightest stars online. Stay tuned!

TIP

mailing list A discussion group that electronically exchanges messages about a particular topic. The mailing list uses a mail exploder so that a message sent to a single address is forwarded to all the people on the list. In a unmoderated list, the mail is forwarded automatically without human intervention or modification. In a moderated list, the mail is first screened by a mod-erator who then forwards mail that is considered appropriate for the group at large. *See also* Usenet, and LISTSERV.

mainframe A large computer that can handle many tasks and interact with many users (through terminals and other devices) at the same time. Mainframes generally require a staff of highly-trained professionals, as opposed to personal computers that can be operated by relatively untrained people. Many of the hosts that you access for files and information on the Internet fit into the category of a mainframe. *See also* minicomputer, and microcomputer.

MAN *See* **Metropolitan Area Network**.

Management Information Base (MIB) A database that maintains information about configuration and performance. An MIB can be on a host, a router, or a bridge. The Simple Network Management Protocol (SNMP) uses an MIB to determine the status and maintain control of network devices.

Manchester encoding A data transmission technology that enables network interface cards to transmit digital signals (0s and 1s) using direct current (DC). The network interface card translates the DC pulses into ASCII characters. Manchester encoding is more reliable than non-return to zero encoding and is used by Ethernet networks.

Marble Teleconnect Nextstep software that enables connection to the Internet via the Serial Line Interface Protocol (SLIP). Developed by Marble Associates.

MARC Machine-Readable Cataloging.

Martian The name given to packets that seem to have fallen out of the sky. Martians are messages that strayed from their intended path because of erroneous routing entries or mangled, incomplete, or just plain wrong Internet addressing.

Matrix 1) A global computer network described in William Gibson's Necromancer. *See also* cyberspace.

2) The network of computers that exchange mail with the Internet but cannot use FTP, telnet, or other services besides mail.

Maximum Transmission Unit (MTU) The longest datagram length that can be sent across a given network.

MB *See* **Megabyte**.

Mbps Megabits (one million bits) per second. *See also* bits per second.

Media Access Control (MAC) A protocol layer that was added between the link layer and the physical layer to define how computers on a LAN can share access to a transmission medium and exchange data.

Megabyte (M or MB) 1,048,576 (or 2^{30}) bytes. Commonly used to measure a computer's storage capacity (for example, 40M) or a high-density floppy disk (1M). Abbreviated to "meg" in conversation, as in "I need one meg to install this emulator."

menu A list of options from which you select. The options can include files and directories (as in Gopher menus). Usually, entering a number selects an option corresponding to that number and moves the user to a new screen or menu with a new set of options.

menu-driven program Software that you manipulate by making selections from a menu, as opposed to entering instructions on command-line or pressing control-characters or clicking on graphical elements (icons) in Macintosh or Windows environments.

TIP

Merit A Michigan Internet provider. For information, send email to jogden@merit.edu.

message cancel A feature of a mail program that gives you a brief window of time in which you can recall a message before it is sent. Invaluable if you type out a nasty-gram before thinking of the consequences. Remember, it's better to retrieve than regret.

message switching *See* **packet switching**.

So You Think You've Been Flamed...

An Internet neophyte had been reading and posting messages to UUCP newsgroups for about a week when she read a vigorously written response to one of her postings. "I think I've been flamed," she said, "but I'm not sure."

continues

continued

The answer is, of course, when you get flamed, you'll know it. For sure. Below are a few choice excerpts from a real, live, official flame (regarding why many foreigners hate America) posted anonymously to (appropriately enough) the `alt.flame` newsgroup.

"You miserable excuse for the offspring of a rat-infested dog turd...didn't they get around to teaching you in your crime-ridden hovel of a University...or were you too busy passing switchblades around in class [that day]?

"This, coming from a denizen of the land that gave us high school metal detectors and talk shows, and put Ronald Reagan in the White House. I submit, you flea-bitten inner-city yahoo, that you would do better to go out and mug some poor old lady than display your ignorance of grammar, your lack of breeding, your utter stupidity, your rhetorical inelegance, your mealy-mouthed parochialism, and your obvious senility in an international forum [such as the Internet].

"Americans are ridiculous. The whole country is ridiculous, starting with that painted tart in New York harbour...the one wearing a dog collar on her head. 'Give me your idiots and morons, the ones too stupid or too obnoxious to make a decent living in the land where they grew up. Give me your...dolts and nitwits, that they may come over here and multiply wondrously and populate the land.'"

∎ ∎ ∎ ∎ ∎ ∎ ∎ ∎ ∎ ∎

Metropolitan Area Network (MAN) A long-distance data network that uses microwave, light beam, or fiber optic technology to interconnect LANs across a city or campus. Not as large a geographical area as a WAN.

MIB *See* **Management Information Base**.

microcomputer A small computer. Micros come in many forms today: desktops, portables, laptops, and notebooks. Also known as a "personal computer" (PC). Today's micros are as fast and powerful as yesterday's mainframes, but they are not on the same order of capacity and processing speed as today's mainframes. *See also* minicomputer, and mainframe.

microprocessor The processing component of an integrated

circuit. It contains the elements for arithmetic, logic, and control. It runs the In/Out basket, receiving instructions from the program in RAM, data from the keyboard, and sending output to the printer. There are many commercial varieties.

mid-level network Regional networks. The concept of "levels" in the Internet is not rigorously defined so this classification is a gray area.

MIDnet A Plains States' U.S. Internet service provider. For information, send email to `dmf@westie.unl.edu`.

mil The domain that includes the U.S. military. For other domains, see "List of Domains."

Military Network (MILNET) The network of military sites that was part of the original ARPANET, the predecessor of the Internet. Non-classified military communications are carried by MILNET. *See also* Advanced Research Projects Agency Network.

MILNET *See* **Military Network**.

MIME *See* **Multipurpose Internet Mail Extensions**.

minicomputer A medium-size computer most often associated with Digital's VAX series of computers. *See also* mainframe, and microcomputer.

MIPS Million instructions per second. A measure of a CPU's capacity.

mirror To reproduce, bit-for-bit, a site located elsewhere on the Internet in a location closer to those who want or need to access the original site. Mirroring a site cuts down on "long-distance" net traffic and creates an entirely new site exactly like the original, which can serve a number of new users.

MNP Microcom Networking Protocol. An error-checking feature that is built into many modems. When using MNP, the modem takes data from your computer, packages it into frames, and transmits the frames to the remote computer. There are various forms of MNP. For example, MNP5 uses a form of data compression that reduces a file by as much as 50 percent.

modeless editor A basic UNIX editor such as ee that does not have a command mode, and therefore everything you type is actually inserted in the document you are editing. You might say a modeless editor has only one modality, and that is the insert mode.

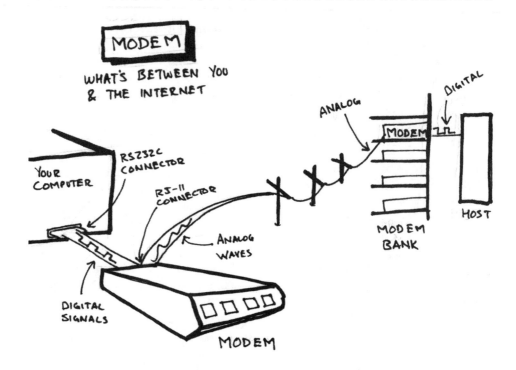

MODEM

WHAT'S BETWEEN YOU & THE INTERNET

YOUR COMPUTER

RS232C CONNECTOR

RJ-11 CONNECTOR

DIGITAL SIGNALS

ANALOG WAVES

MODEM

ANALOG

DIGITAL

MODEM

MODEM BANK

HOST

modem A device that acts as the electronic go-between in the marriage of telephone and computer. It converts a computer's digital pulse into an analog tone that can be transmitted over a telephone line. It also performs the reverse conversion. "Modem" is a blend of modulation/demodulation. Modem speed is measured in bits per second. Modems range in performance from the original Bell 103 modem which clomped along at 300 bps to the 57,600 bps modems used to connect to network providers over leased lines. The typical Internet user goes netfaring via a 2,400 to 14,400 bps modem. *See also* digital, analog, and carrier.

modem bank A specialized set of shelves on which several modems can be stacked so they can be conveniently connected to a terminal server.

moderated list A mailing list that has a moderator who volunteers to screen messages for appropriateness before posting them to the general readership. Convenient, but faintly Orwellian. *Contrast* unmoderated list.

moderator In a moderated mailing list, this person reads postings to the list to make sure they comply with the group's guidelines for appropriateness. Often, a moderator will, rather than screen each message, simply monitor the discussions on an unmoderated list and make comments to the list's members urging them to stick to the topic at hand or avoid making

rash and inflammatory comments and so forth.

monospaced font A typeface that produces characters of equal width. The typical word processing program today routinely works with a variety of proportional fonts (characters that vary in width), but these fonts do not translate well from one computer to another in terms of line length (the distance between margins). When you compose email messages and text files to be sent over the Internet, it is recommended that you limit the line length to 80 characters. This is the maximum viewable space for most terminal screens and emulators. However, you should use a monospace font when you are setting line length so that you are actually sending 80 characters. Monospaced fonts for the Macintosh are Monaco and Courier.

MOO *See* **Multi-User Dungeon**.

Morning Star PPP Nextstep software that enables connection to the Internet via the Point-to-Point Protocol (PPP). Developed by Morning Star Technologies.

Mosaic Graphically oriented software that enables you to browse and search the World-Wide Web. Mosaic runs on Mac, Windows, and UNIX platforms and employs a main window with a built-in search field and menus to enable you to easily retrieve items for viewing. Requires additional

software for Serial Line Interface Protocol (SLIP) connection. Mosaic has become incredibly popular because it is easy to use, graphically appealing, and powerful both as a search tool and as a browsing aid for exploring or "spelunking" the Internet. Available by anonymous FTP at `ftp.ncsa.uiuc.edu`.

Motion Picture Experts Group (MPEG) A committee working under the International Standards Organization (ISO) that has proposed a universal standard for the compression and decompression of motion video and audio.

POTATO EVOLUTION

1. COUCH

2. MOUSE

MPEG *See* **Motion Picture Experts Group**.

mouse potato A net junkie who spends every waking moment surfing the Internet. Note that a mouse is optional for net-surfing, although the term may be applied to any so-called basement-dwelling troglodyte who has seemingly put down roots into the seat in front of the computer terminal.

mpeg File extension for MPEG-compressed animation.

MRNet (Minnesota Regional Network) A Minnesota Internet provider. For information, send email to info@mr.net.

MSEN A Michigan Internet provider. For information, contact info@msen.com.

MTU *See* **Maximum Transmission Unit**.

MUD, MUSE, MUSH, *See* **Multi-User Dungeon**.

TIP

Multi-User Dungeon (MUD) The Internet isn't just for serious scholarly pursuits. You can also play games. Using telnet, you can participate in online role-playing games that fall under the general heading of "MUDs" or Mucks, or Muses, or Mushes, or MOOs (sometimes called "tiny muds"). MUD can also stand for Multi-User Dimension. These are fantasy games in which the players take on different roles often in different environments or worlds. Although to play these games you really just type in text in an interactive talk session format, players often speak of these imaginative adventures as "virtual reality " and take them quite seriously. To start out, see the Usenet news group: rec.games.mud.announce. Then telnet into the world of your choice.

Slogging through the MUDs

Finding your way around the scores of MUDs on the Net can be a daunting task at first. If you're interested in exploring the world of MUDs, keep in mind that it's all in fun, and don't worry about picking up on every detail your first time out.

Here are a few resources to help you get started on your quest for MUD fulfillment:

Check the newsgroups rec.games.mud.announce and alt.mud for information on the newest MUDs.

For a list of scores of MUDs, FTP to `caisr2.caisr.cwru.edu` and check the `/pub/mud/` directory.

For a wide array of general information on MUDs, including MUD lists, data on other MUD ftp sites and special software for navigating MUDs, FTP to `actlab.rtf.utexas.edu`.

M

Multiple Virtual Storage (MVS) An IBM mainframe operating system that is parallel to, but distinct from, Virtual Machine (VM).

multiplexing One of those great techie-nerd words that simply means a lot of lines going into one channel or pipe.

Multipurpose Internet Mail Extensions An improvement over straight-text email, MIME enables the transfer of formatted text, color pictures, video, and sound in addition to routine messages.

Multipurpose Internet Mail Extensions (MIME) A protocol for Internet email that enables the transmission of nontextual data such as graphics, audio, video and other binary types of files.

multitasking A computer that switches between operations so quickly it appears to be doing several things at once. Some people engage in the human equivalent of multitasking (and actually do it with some proficiency) while others are better suited to a more linear, single-task method.

MVS *See* **Multiple Virtual Storage**.

MX Record *See* **Mail Exchange Record**.

nagware Shareware that comes with a pesky little screen that pops up to remind you to register (shareware marketing lingo for "pay for") your copy of the program.

NAK *See* **Negative Acknowledgment**.

Name Binding Protocol (NBP) The AppleTalk Transport level protocol that translates between numeric AppleTalk addresses and alphanumeric names of entities. NBP responds to requests for location by referencing a table it maintains that lists nodes and corresponding named entities.

TIP

NAND The Boolean operator meaning "not and." When you place NAND in a database search request, the datebase will not return items that have both terms. You use NAND to cut down the number of returned items by eliminating items that meet two conditions simultaneously. For instance, if you have a database subset of all articles about the Olympics and you want to eliminate articles about skiing gold medalists, you could enter "SKIING NAND GOLD".

National Information Standards Organization (NISO) The organization that has revised Z39.50—the standard on which WAIS is based.

National Institute of Standards and Technology (NIST) U.S. governmental organization that supports the development of national standards. Formerly the National Bureau of Standards.

National Public Telecommunications Network (NPTN) A nonprofit network based in Cleveland, OH committed to making computer networking available to as many people as possible through freenets.

National Research and Education Network (NREN) The network envisioned by Vice President Al Gore and the High-Performance Computing Act of 1991. Eventually, NREN will be the American electronic superhighway connecting schools, research facilities, and government agencies.

National Science Foundation (NSF) The U.S. Government agency that funded NSFNET and many of the university connections to the Internet. NSF's primary mission is to promote science and finance scientific projects and facilities.

natural language query A method of searching a database using everyday, non-technical words instead of obscure commands. A natural language is one that evolved over time through usage by people such as English or Spanish, as opposed to an artificial language that was developed for computers. *See also* Wide Area Information Server (WAIS). A natural language query might read like: "Find all information about agricultural exports from Chile."

navigator Graphical software that enables you to browse through the various services provided by online information providers. In the specific sense, Navigator is the name of the graphical navigation software for use with CompuServe.

NBP *See* **Name Binding Protocol**.

NCSA Telnet Macintosh telnet sofware. Available by anonymous FTP at sumex-aim.stanford.edu.

net druids
Hardware sorcerers who control the silicon that makes the Internet work. While druids technically rank below heavies on the ladder of net influence, they have more direct power over the Internet because of their mystical knowledge of how the Net actually works. They are a secretive group that practices arcane and sometimes frightening rituals to honor the net gods, and are believed to be a branch of the freemasons.

NEARNET *See* **New England Academic and Research Network**.

NEARnet A Northeastern U.S. Internet provider. For information, send email to nearnet-join@nic.near.net.

Negative Acknowledgment (NAK) Sent by a network device when a block of data sent has not been received successfully. A NAK is triggered when the checksum value calculated from the transmitted data differs from the checksum value of the received data. *See also* checksum. *Contrast* ACK.

Net News Transport Protocol (NNTP) The transmission protocol used in the dissemination of Usenet news.

net The domain that includes network resources.

net heavies System administrators who honcho big sites.

net news Messages in a Usenet news group.

Netaddress *See* **Knowbot Information Services**.

Netcom Online Communication Services A California Internet provider. For information, send email to ruthann@netcom.com.

netcropper A technically proficient Internet enthusiast hoodwinked, enslaved, or otherwise obligated to fulfill the cash-rich dreams of a carpetnetter—a marketing wizard or other robber baron of the infoscape. *See also* carpetnetter.

 TIP

netIllinois An Illinois Internet provider. For information, send email to `joel@bradley.edu`.

netiquette Network etiquette. *See also* Internetiquette.

net anxiety A condition suffered by hardcore net-dwellers wherein they feel extreme anxiety, worry,

and agitation when unable to log onto the Internet for protracted periods of time.

You Say Tomato, I Say Cultural Imperialism

Because the Internet is truly the world's first global communication forum, you never know who's "listening" to what you "say". Consequently, you never know who you're likely to offend with a particular comment or statement.

If an infinite number of monkeys plinking at an infinite number of typewriters will eventually tap out the complete works of Shakespeare, the odds are strong that a single user typing at a single terminal will immediately invoke the wrath of at least one of the Net's near-infinite inhabitants.

But even if it's impossible to keep from assaulting the sensibilities of everyone on the Net, it certainly helps to keep the proper perspective on the Internet as a town crier that reaches every corner of the global village.

During a discussion on the Internet's role as a tool for reaching folks around the world, one participant wrote, "Consider the Internet as a tool for exporting American ideology. It's going to make Hollywood look like a *samizdat* of home movies by the turn of the century."

Terry Smith of Australia read that posting and politely suggested a somewhat more globally enlightened perspective on the Internet's power to communicate opinions throughout world: "I've got a better idea. Consider it a tool for importing other viewpoints."

TIP

NetManage Chameleon Software that enables you to install TCP/IP on your PC and connect to the Internet via a LAN or dial-up with SLIP or PPP. There are versions for Windows, DOS, and Windows NT. Developed by NetManage, Inc.

Netnews *See* **Usenet**.

Network File System (NFS) A UNIX system presentation layer protocol developed by Sun Microsystems that enables you to use files and directories stored on another computer as though they were stored on the local computer. You can read, write, and edit files to the remote computer without using FTP to transfer the files to your local computer. You can read it, write it, or edit it on the remote computer—using the same commands that you'd use locally. More than 200 companies have used this protocol in their products.

Network Information Center (NIC) An organization that provides information, assistance, and administrative services to users of a network. The NIC oversees network names and addresses and is often a repository of RFCs. The Internet has its own NIC called "InterNIC," of course. Sometimes, you'll see a reference to "the NIC," which is usually a reference to the

Defense Data Network Network Information Center.

Network Layer Layer three of the OSI Reference Model defines the protocols for data routing and the addressing standards for sender and recipient. IP is the network layer for TCP/IP networks. DDP is the network layer for AppleTalk networks.

Network News Transfer Protocol (NNTP) A protocol that specifies how news articles are to be distributed, queried, retrieved, and posted.

Network Operations Center (NOC) A group responsible for taking care of a network. This involves monitoring operations and responding to connection breaks. If you can't access a network, these are the people you talk to. *See also* Network Information Center.

Network Time Protocol (NTP) A protocol that enables clocks to be sychronized on the Internet with reference to radio and atomic clocks.

network A group of computers or other devices connected for the purpose of exchanging data and sharing resources. Networks enable computers to share files, electronic mail systems, communication links to other networks, and printers. A network can consist of any combination of LANs, MANs, or WANs, although generally such combinations are called "internets" or "internetworks." *See also* LAN, WAN.

network interface card (or controller) (nic)
Network interface card (or controller). An adapter card that is installed in a PC enabling it to connect to a network. There is a specific nic for each type of network (for example, Ethernet, Token Ring). The card contains both the hardware to accommodate the network's cables and the software to employ the network's protocols. The nic takes the data from the computer and packages it to be sent out on the network. It controls the data streaming between the internal data bus and the network cable. Computers either have a built-in nic or have one added to the expansion bus. Some nics attach to the computer's parallel port. Also called a "LAN adapter."

network operating system (NOS)
A suite of programs that run on networked computers. Typically, a network operating system provides the capability of sharing files, printers, and other resources in the network. Client and server software are usually part of a NOS.

network peripheral
Devices, such as printers and modems, that connect directly to networks rather than being attached to computers. A network peripheral has a built-in processor to run server software.

New England Academic and Research Network (NEARNET) A regional provider of Internet services. For information, send email to `nearnet-join@nic.near.net`.

news Short for Usenet news.

news reader A program that assists in sorting out the articles generated by Usenet newsgroups by enabling you to select newsgroups and articles, usually by following or deleting threads. Examples include rn, nn, trn, and tin. There are a number of graphical news readers for Macintosh and Windows computers with a SLIP connection or better.

newsfeed A source of news that is sent through networks. ClariNet and Usenet are both receivers and transmitters of the news being fed to them.

newsgroup *See* **Usenet Newsgroups**.

NeXT-WAIStation Nextstep software that enables you to search WAIS through a graphical interface. Also makes a WAIS server out of a Nextstep computer. Available by anonymous FTP at `sonata.cc.purdue.edu`.

`newsrc` A file created by UNIX news-readers showing the news groups in which you are interested. Each line of the newsrc file has the name of a single news group terminated by a colon. For example: `soc.culture.portuguese:`, `rec.games.pinball:`, and `rec.radio.shortwave:`¨Á

Nextstep An Intel-based PC operating system that adds a graphical interface to UNIX.

NFS *See* **Network File System**.

nibble Half a byte, either the first four or last four bits of a byte.

NIC *See* **Network Information Center**.

nic *See* **network interface card (or controller)**.

nic.ddn.mil The domain name of the Defense Data Network NIC.

nickname *See* **alias**.

Nikenet *See* **sneakernet**.

NIS *See* **Network Information Services**.

NISO *See* **National Information Standards Organization**.

NIST *See* **National Institute of Standards and Technology**.

NLnet A Newfoundland and Labrador Internet provider.

nn UNIX news reader.

NNTP *See* **Network News Transfer Protocol**.

No Carrier The message relayed to you by your modem when the connection breaks between your modem and the remote computer. *See also* carrier.

NOC *See* **Network Operations Center**.

Nodal Switching System (NSS) The major routing nodes of the NSFNET backbone.

node In a computer network, any physical device, such as a computer or printer, that can be addressed by other devices. Synonymous with "device" in anything other than a highly technical context.

nodename The name of a device connected to a network that is given a unique address.

non-interactive An automated approach to message retrieval. Rather than reading messages one-at-a-time, you can use a program that retrieves the email without your personal interaction. *Contrast* interactive.

non-return to zero (NRZ) A basic encoding method that uses two separate voltage levels, one positive and one negative, to represent binary digits (0s and 1s). With NRZ, it is difficult to tell the boundary between one bit and another. NRZ is less reliable than Manchester encoding.

■■■■■■■■ **TIP** ■■■■■■■■

NorthWest Net A Northwestern U.S. Internet provider. For information, send email to ehood@nwnet.net.

■■■■■■■■■■■■■■■■■■■■■■

NOS *See* **network operating system**.

NOT The Boolean operator used to limit searches to strings that contain one term, but not another. For example, the string "george NOT washington" will return a list of Georges that do not include George Washington.

NPTN *See* **National Public Tele-communications Network**.

NREN *See* **National Research and Education Network**.

NRZ *See* **non-return to zero**.

NSF *See* **National Science Foundation**.

NSFNET One of the Internet's primary backbone networks. NSFNET connects 16 nodes, including five supercomputers, in academic and research facilities across the country. The main trunk operates at 45M bps and connects several regional networks.

NSS *See* **Nodal Switching System**.

NSTN A Nova Scotia, Canada, Internet provider. For information, send email to `parsons@hawk.nstn.ns.ca`.

NTP *See* **Network Time Protocol**.

numeric string A group of values that can be used in numeric operations.

Nuntius Macintosh graphical newsreader software that that runs in conjunction with a Net News Transport Protocol (NNTP) news server. Available by anonymous FTP at `sumex-aim.stanford.edu`.

NUPop Windows newsreader software that runs in conjunction with a Net News Transport Protocol (NNTP) news server. Available by anonymous FTP at `ftp.acns.nwu.edu`.

NVE *See* **Network-Visible Entity**.

NYSERNet A New York Internet provider. For information, send email to `luckett@nysernet.org`.

TIP

OARnet An Ohio Internet provider. For information, send email to alison@osc.eud.

OBI *See* **Online Book Initiative**.

OCLC *See* **Online Computer Library Center**.

octet An 8-bit quantity. In networking discussions, octet is often preferred to "byte" because some computers have been designed that use bytes of some length other than eight bits. Most of the time, you are safe in using either of these terms. In certain contexts, some writers prefer logical byte to either octet or byte.

odd parity *See* **parity**.

offline 1) Said of a device that may be connected to another computer or network, but is not ready to respond to requests. Most printers have an "online-offline" toggle button (it may have a name such as "Select"). If you take a printer "offline," it will not process print jobs that are sent to it. While it is in "offline" mode, you can add paper to the tray or make adjustments such as changing the orientation from portrait to landscape printing. Taking a printer "offline" is different than turning it off.

2) Said of a person who is not actively communicating over a network. Someone who has logged off an interactive talk session is "offline."

3) In computer slang, "offline" means you're not at full functioning capacity.

4) Another use of "offline" is to indicate that you want to discuss an issue in different circumstances. "I'll answer that offline," is a glib way of dodging a question asked in public that you would prefer to answer in private.

Contrast online.

ohm A measurement of how much a transmission medium resists a flow of electrons, or current, passing through it. A unit equals the resistance of a circuit in which a potential difference of one volt produces a current of one ampere. Named after Georg Simon Ohm. *See also* impedance and resistance.

ohmmeter A device that measures voltages and resistance.

OIC Oh, I see! A common shorthand abbreviation seen in chat sessions and email messages.

Oldie A Delphi text editor.

Onet An Ontario, Canada Internet provider. For information, send email to eugene@vm.utcs.utoronto.ca.

Online Book Initiative™ (OBI) An organization that uses the Internet to disseminate material that is not currently copyrighted. Some of the literature has never been copyrighted, some of it had been copyrighted at one time. You can reach OPI by anonymous FTP at world.std.com. *See also* Project Gutenberg.

Online Computer Library Center (OCLC) A nonprofit organization of more than 10,000 interconnected libraries that provide computer-based services for libraries and educational organizations. The OCLC system provides cataloging, interlibrary loan, collection development, and reference services. OCLC operates the FirstSearch Catalog through which library users can access dozens of databases including the U.S. Printing Office "Monthly Catalog," the "Readers' Guide to Periodical Literature," as well as business and scientific journals. To

learn more about the OCLC offerings, subscribe to the FirstSearch mailing list at listserv@oclc.org.

online 1) Said of a device that is currently connected to another computer or network and is ready to respond to requests. A printer that is ready to print a file sent to it is "online."

2) Said of a person who is actively communicating over a network. "Online" in this sense means your computer is connected to a network host or service and you can participate in Internet activities such as discussion groups or interactive talk sessions.

3) Online is the time you are charged for if you're connected to a fee-based Internet service.

4) In computer slang, "online" means you're awake and functioning.

Contrast offline.

online information service A commercial organization that provides a variety of electronic services such as forums, email, games, and connections to databases. Some of them, such as Delphi and America Online, provide gateways to the Internet. Some do not, such as Prodigy and CompuServe. All of them exchange email to some extent with Internet users.

Has the Internet Gone to the Dogs?

While it's usually a good idea to make sure your name is attached to anything you post on the Net or email to a fellow netizen (unsigned electronic correspondence generally carries the same weight—none— as it does in paper form), there are specific instances where it's better to remain anonymous.

A cartoon in *The New Yorker* showed a dog typing away at a computer terminal with the caption below reading, "On the Internet, no one knows you're a dog." That's part of the beauty of the Net, and if you have something to say that demands anonymity, there's a way you can say it online without folks knowing who you are.

There are various servers around the Net that will allow you to post anonymous messages to newsgroups, and even receive replies (anonymous or otherwise) without anyone knowing your real name or email address. While this might mean you could receive mail from a man pretending to be a woman, a mechanic masquerading as a doctor, or a physics professor claiming to be a nine-year-old video game whiz, you can be reasonably sure your dog won't be emailing you...yet.

For information on using an anonymous posting service, send email to `help@anon.penet.fi`.

■ ■ ■ ■ ■ ■ ■ ■ ■ ■

Open Software Foundation (OSF) A consortium formed by Digital, IBM, and Hewlett-Packard.

Open Systems Interconnection (OSI) An international program sponsored by the International Organization for Standardization (IOS) to create computer communication standards, including the OSI Reference Model. The U.S. government has mandated OSI as a standard to be gradually implemented for computer equipment. *See also* Government OSI Profile (GOSIP).

open protocols Protocols that can be applied to a variety of manufacturers, not just one.

operating system The basic software instructions that make a box of electronic parts into a computer humans can interact with. On the Internet, the hosts you access have a variety of operating systems. The three most dominant proprietary operating systems are UNIX, IBM's VM, and Digital's VMS. The screen displays, menus, prompts, and commands vary considerably from system to system.

option A choice on a menu.

TIP

OR A Boolean operator used to expand searches to include items that meet any one of two or more criteria. For example, if you're searching for information on Napolean's strategy at Waterloo, you don't necessarily want to limit your search to only those articles that deal with Waterloo. His patterns as a military leader are also of interest, along with the specifics of Waterloo. Consequently, you might search for "Napolean OR Waterloo," which would yield articles containing either the word "Napolean" or the word "Waterloo."

org The domain that includes organizations other than the military, government, or educational institutions. Usually, an "org" is a non-commercial, non-government organization, often a non-profit group, such as the Electronic Frontier Foundation.

OSF *See* **Open Software Foundation**.

OSF/1 A version of UNIX that runs on a VAX.

OSI *See* **Open Systems Interconnection**.

OSI Reference Model A seven-layer model that describes the standard protocols established by the ISO for interconnecting dissimilar computers and networks. (OSI stands for Open Systems Interconnection.) It was developed in 1978. The seven layers, (with layer seven at the top) are:

Layer	*Defines Standards For ...*
Application	Interaction between applications and communication services
Presentation	File formats and file access formats
Session	Making and maintaining a logical connection
Transport	Control of the delivery of information
Network	Data routing and addressing
Data Link	Data frames and transmission
Physical	Cabling and communications medium

For more information about each, consult the individual entries.

OSPF *See* **Open Shortest-Path First Interior Gateway Protocol**.

OTF On the Floor. A common shorthand abbreviation seen in chat sessions and email messages.

OTOH On the Other Hand. A common shorthand abbreviation seen in chat sessions and email messages.

OTTH On the Third Hand. A common shorthand abbreviation seen in chat sessions and email messages.

Outernet Those networks and bulletin boards that can interact with Internet through gateways. AppleLink, CompuServe, MCI Mail, and UUCP networks are joined in the Outernet by hundreds of others.

overhead Protocol information that is added to the data being transmitted. In order to insure the accurate delivery of data, protocols add information into headers and trailers. This extra "baggage" performs a valuable function, but is sometimes considered unnecessary. "Overhead" is an accounting term and it is appropriately applied here, because the deluxe protocols add costs in the form of additional bandwidth and time. *See also* throughput.

PACCOM A Pacific Rim and Hawaiian Internet provider. For information, send email to torben@hawaii.edu.

TIP

Packet InterNet Groper (PING) A program that sends a signal to a network device to determine if a connection can be made. The signal is an Internet Control Message Protocol (ICMP) echo that waits for a reply. By sending a PING command, you can determine if a printer is online or just out of paper. The format is PING device name. Think of PING as an electronic Joan Rivers asking: "Can we talk?"

Packet Switch Node (PSN) The computer that routes packets in a packet-switched network.

packet A generic term to refer to the organized, discrete bundles of data that are transported across networks. The packet of bits contains address, data, and control information that are switched and transmitted together. In informal usage, "packet" is an adequate word, but not always technically accurate. A TCP "packet" is a segment; an IP "packet" is a datagram. Packets are usually less than 1500 bytes long. Anything longer is broken into a packet before being transported and then reassembled at the receiving computer.

packet sniffer An electronic wire tapper. Applied to either a person or a program that seeks out information in an unauthorized way.

packet-switched network In this arrangement, all the nodes of the network share a common link simultaneously and pass packets of information to each other. Each packet, labeled with the addresses of sender and receiver, advances from node to node until it reaches its intended destination. The Internet uses TCP/IP to disassemble, transmit, and reassemble packets. Included in this category are most LANs as well as X.25, frame-relay, and cell-relay networks. *See also* public-data networks. *Contrast* circuit-switched network.

Packetized Ensemble Protocol (PEP) A method of connecting two modems to increase transfer of data. A proprietary feature offered by Telebit.

PAP *See* **Printer Access Protocol**.

parallel More than one thing in the same direction at the same time. In data transmission, parallel means that all the bits that make up a character can be sent simultaneously on parallel electrical channels. *Contrast* serial, where the bits are sent sequentially.

parallel port A socket on the back of a computer where you can attach a cable to interface with a parallel device (for example, a printer) that accepts several bits of data over separate wires simultaneously. *Compare* serial port.

parity A method for detecting errors in data transmission that adds an extra bit to each character string (or byte). In even parity, if the total of the bits that make up a single character does not add up to an even number, the transmitter adds a "1" in the parity bit field. The data is then sent. The receiver repeats the sum. If the result is not "even," then an error has occurred. "Odd" parity is an identical process except the sum of the bits is an odd number.

passive star A network laid out in a star shape with every branch leading to a common point. The star is said to be "passive" because there is no repeater at the center to actively retransmit signals. *Contrast* active star. *See also* star topology.

patch A correction that (hopefully) fixes a bug, but as its name implies, this is not a permanent solution. Fringeware can be said to be

patched together, and some would include well-known commercial packages as well.

PC Eudora Windows mail manager software that runs in conjunction with an Internet Post Office Protocol (POP) server. Available by anonymous FTP at `ftp.qualcomm.com`.

PC Gopher for DOS PC Gopher client software. Available by anonymous FTP at `sunsite.unc.edu`.

PC Pursuit A service offered by SprintNet that enables you to directly connect to a computer (as opposed to SprintNet which connects you to an online information service). Useful for connecting to Internet access providers, bulletin board systems, and individual computers. Uses the same 600 local phone numbers as SprintNet.

PC-Xware Windows software that provides TCP/IP, X server access for X Window applications, NFS, and FTP. Developed by Network Computing Devices, Inc.

PC/TCP Plus for DOS DOS software that enables you to dial-up computers on the Internet so that you can use FTP and telnet. Developed by FTP Software.

PD Public Domain.

PDIAL *See* **Public Dialup Internet Access List**.

PDN *See* **Public Data Network**.

PDU *See* **Protocol Data Unit**.

peer A network device that communicates on the same level as another device on the network.

PEM *See* **Privacy-Enhanced Mail**.

PEP *See* **Packetized Ensemble Protocol**.

Performance Systems International (PSI) A worldwide Internet provider. For information, send email to `info@psi.com`.

peripheral Originally, a device external to the CPU of the mainframe: printers, tape drives, etc. Now, with the popularity of LAN's, almost anything is a peripheral of something else.

Let's Get Personal

When the mainstream media is searching for a sensational angle on the information highway to jazz up the 11 o'clock news, reporters and producers remember that old adage of advertising (and apparently television journalism in the 90s): sex sells!

Whether it's a smirking local anchor, a bombastic tabloid reporter, or a probing Oprahldo-style talk show host, cybersex is the favorite variation of the all-too-familiar puff pieces about the Internet.

While virtual sex, robot sex, digital sex, and other high-tech sex-schemes make for interesting headlines, most of the sex fostered by the Internet seems to be taking place within that well-tested model of two (or more) people.

The Net is full or personal ads (many posted anonymously) ranging from folks looking for pen pals or buddies to share coffee or a movie with, to relationships of a rather more adventurous nature, such as the one outlined in the anonymous personal ad below.

"I will be driving across the country from NYC to L.A. over the summer. I am looking for encounters with males, females, or couples along the way. I am hoping to fulfill my own and other's dreams as I go. If anyone is interested in being with this attractive 21-year old, let me know so we can make arrangements."

■ ■ ■ ■ ■ ■ ■ ■ ■ ■

PGP Pretty Good Privacy is public-domain encryption software developed by Phillip Zimmerman. Unlike other encryption schemes such as the Clipper Chip and SKIPJACK, Zimmerman's PGP does not use encryption algorithms that have been "endorsed" by the National Security Council, which means documents or files encrypted via PGP are probably safer from the prying eyes of the NSA (or anyone else) than if they were encrypted using any other system.

Physical Layer Layer one (the bottom) of the OSI Reference Model. It defines the protocols for the physical cabling or delivery medium (for example, Ethernet and Token Ring cables).

physical Adjective applied to hardware of all kinds—computers, drivers, modems, and connecting media. When in doubt, "physical" is anything you can touch. *Contrast* logical.

pico A UNIX text editor that comes with the Pine email program but which can also run separately.

Pine A UNIX email program that is easier to use than UNIX mail.

PING *See* **Packet InterNet Groper**.

pipe Slang for any cable or wire, whether twisted-pair, fiber optic, or T1.

pit File extension for a Macintosh PackIt file. PackIt is an old compression program and is not in widespread use any more.

PITA Pain in the Ass. A common shorthand abbreviation seen in chat sessions and email messages.

pixel The basic element of an image (analogous to a bit, the basic element of data). A blend of the words picture and element. Coined in 1969.

pkg File extension for an AppleLink Package file.

plan file *See* **finger**.

Point-to-Point Protocol (PPP) A TCP/IP protocol for transmitting IP datagrams over serial lines such as dialup phone lines. PPP performs the same function as SLIP; however, it operates on the link layer and is slightly faster than SLIP. Both the remote host and the local computer must have PPP installed. PPP is considered to be a successor to SLIP, but if the remote host does not have PPP installed, you must connect via SLIP.

POP *See* **Post Office Protocol** and **Point Of Presence**.

port (Noun) 1) A socket on the back of a computer for plugging in cables for modems, printers, or other devices.

2) Any male or female connector for interfacing computers and peripherals.

3) On network hosts, a specific channel where a program runs that is given a unique number. System administrators can set this up to control access. Packets sent from one computer to another contain information about the application, which is identified by a port number.

On some systems, you can telnet directly to a program rather than connecting to the host first and then launching the program. Sometimes you will need to do this if you want to use a specific program that is generally available to the public on a host that is otherwise private. By telneting directly to the program via the port number, you will not be asked for a user ID and password. To access such a program, you simply add the port number to the normal host name. For example, to reach port 600 on a server at Rutgers you would telnet to `rutgers.edu 600`.

4) The interface between a router and a network.

(Verb) To convert software code so that it can run on a computer that is different than the one for which the code was originally developed.

Portal Communications A San Francisco Bay Internet provider with worldwide access through Sprint. For more information, send email to `info@portal.com`.

Post Office Protocol (POP) A protocol that specifies exchanges of email between a personal computer and an access provider's computer. POP enables users with client software on their computers to read mail from a server.

post To send an electronic message to a newsgroup or mailing list.

posting An article sent to a discussion group newsgroup or mailing list.

postmaster A mail program administrator who responds to email problems for an individual site. If there is a problem, you may get a message with a subject such as: "Undeliverable mail: SMTP delivery failure." The message may cite an error condition such as "Illegal host/domain name not found." If you're totally confused and frustrated, try sending an email addressed to "postmaster."

PostScript A proprietary computer language developed by Adobe Systems. It describes the formatting of text and graphics with mathematical precision. The commands cannot be viewed on screen and are only interpreted by PostScript devices. PostScript is made up of 7-bit characters so it can be transmitted over the Internet without encoding. The usual file extension for a PostScript file found in directories is "ps."

PPP *See* **Point-to-Point Protocol**.

PREPnet A Pennsylvania Internet provider. For information send email to twb+@andrew.cmu.edu.

Presentation Layer Layer six of the OSI Reference Model defines the protocols for file formats and file access formats.

Printer Access Protocol (PAP) The AppleTalk protocol that specifies communication set-up, data transfer and connection termination functions that occur between a workstation and a printer or print servers.

Privacy Enhanced Mail (PEM) Email that uses encryption methods to provide confidentiality, authentication, and message integrity.

Private Virtual Circuit (PVC) Software-based circuits that enable you to have a private line between two sites.

privileges 1) Generally, a set of computer, network, or directory activities to which a user is specifically entitled. Privileges are also called "rights."

2) Specifically, a user's rights to use directories and files.

The system administrator assigns privileges to individuals, groups, and everyone.

3) Specifically, a method of limiting and controlling how an individual uses a computer or network. This is usually called "access privileges." There are normally levels of privileges, and users are given usernames and passwords to access certain systems, hosts, or applications. On the network level, system administrators set policies for access; at the desktop level, individual users can control access through software packages such as Disk Lock for the Macintosh. *See also* anonymous FTP.

Procomm Plus A popular telecommunications program for IBM-compatible PCs. Datastorm Technologies, Inc., Columbia, MO.

Prodigy America's largest online service with two million subscribers does not have a connection to the Internet, but its users are able to exchange email with Internet users.

PROFS Professional Office System. An IBM calendar and email program that runs in a VM environment. PROFS came to national attention during the Iran-Contra hearings when it was learned that Oliver North and his associates communicated using PROFS email, unwittingly leaving an electronic trail of their stratagems. North thought he had erased all incriminating email messages, but had not, in fact, eradicated all vestiges of his online communications.

Project Gutenberg An organization that uses the Internet to disseminate books that are not currently copyrighted. Project Gutenberg collects

some older books that have not been copyrighted for some time. Other items in its inventory, such as census reports, have never been copyrighted. You can reach them via anonymous FTP at mrcnext. cso.uiuc.edu. *See also* Online Book Initiative.

Downloaded Any Good Books Lately?

It doesn't seem likely that the book as we know it will be supplanted by computer versions any time in the near future. After all, books don't need batteries, can survive a day at the beach, or a week stuck in the back window of a station wagon. They don't need RAM upgrades, they won't crash when the network goes down, and you'll never hear anyone complain about wasting an entire afternoon optimizing and defragmenting the New Testament.

But having books in electronic form is undoubtedly helpful for a number of reasons. You can quickly and easily search for specific words, copy passages for quotes and commentary, and create your own large print edition in any typeface you like.

While a number of companies from tiny start-ups to huge media conglomerates scramble to create mega-media book experiences, a number of folks on the Net are quietly moving mountains as part of a massive effort to convert to digital (usually ASCII) format thousands of public-domain works ranging from Shakespeare to Mark Twain to *The Federalist Papers*.

Project Gutenberg texts are available from various FTP sites throughout the Net.

project file *See* **finger**.

prompt 1) A question or request for information or action that is displayed on your screen by a host computer. Here are some typical examples: USENET-HELP>(Enter Number, Scan, "?" or Exit):, More?, and Press Return.

2) The character or symbol that shows the command line area. This varies considerably from host to host depending on the operating system and local preferences.

Prompt	Shell
>UNIX	Tenex C-Shell
%UNIX	C-Shell
bash$UNIX	Bourne Again Shell
$Bourne	Shell and Korn Shell

Prospero A distributed directory system, file system, and index service. You can use Prospero to create a virtual file system incorporating both local and remote directories. Prospero also enables you to access files using anonymous FTP and the Network File System (NFS). Archie uses the Prospero protocol.

protocol layers The architectural elements of a protocol. A layered model provides a simple framework for developing procedures and solutions. Carrying data across great geographical and technological distances is a complex business. There are many diverse functions involved, from formatting and packaging the data to determining the route it will take. Separating the different communication functions into parts, or layers, makes it easy to work on. Furthermore, when you make a change on one layer, the other layers are insulated from the changes. For example, the Ethernet protocol affecting wiring was amended to allow for unshielded twisted-pair. This did not affect the other protocol layers. The TCP/IP suite has five layers of protocols, while the OSI Reference model has seven.

protocol stack A set of protocols that together provide communications between applications. TCP, IP, and Ethernet constitute a protocol stack.

protocol suite A group of protocols that work together to provide a range of functions. For example, the TCP/IP suite contains Transmission Control Protocol (TCP), Internet Protocol (IP), File Transfer Protocol (FTP), Simple Mail Transfer Protocol (SMTP), Telnet, and Domain Name Systems (DNS) directory services, among others.

Sometimes "family" is substituted for "suite."

protocols Rules and conventions without which nothing would work, especially computers exchanging data. By mutually agreeing to use common procedures and formats, computers made by different vendors can "talk" to each other and share resources. Protocols form the logical bridges between diverse technologies and govern each element of data communications. The point of the Internet—and all networks—is to enable one computer to exchange information with another. And to do that effectively, both computers must agree on a long list of details, such as how to sequence the bits for transmission, what information to put in the header, how to format email messages, and how to ensure that all the data sent out is received intact and in the right order. While a network doesn't require that all players necessarily sing exactly the same tune, they must all be in the same key, and protocols provide the sheet music.

A protocol suite or family, refers to the entire set of protocols used by a particular network. No single protocol in the suite is sufficient on its own; they all work together, each handling a part.

A protocol stack refers to the specific way the protocol suite is implemented on a particular computer.

ps The file extension for PostScript files.

PSCnet An Eastern U.S. Internet provider. For information, send email to `hastings@psu.edu`.

PSI *See* **Performance Systems International**.

PSN *See* **Packet Switch Node**.

Public Data Network (PDN) A category of packet-switching networks that are commercial and offer a high degree of error-control, buffering, and protocol conversion. Included in this are Tymnet, SprintNet, PC Pursuit, and CompuServe Packet Network.

Public Dialup Internet Access List (PDIAL) A list of Internet service providers offering public access dialup accounts. These providers have Internet access for FTP, Telnet, and other services. Some also provide email and Usenet newsfeed. PDIAL is copyrighted by Peter Kaminski, but it "may be copied freely for non-commercial use if not modified."

I Want My PGP!

If you follow the encryption game—or even if you don't—you're probably aware of the flap over the proposed Clipper Chip encryption scheme proposed by various U.S. government agencies and backed by the Clinton Administration (*see* "Clipping the Wings of Encryption Liberty," page 64).

In short, if you don't currently own a secure encryption program, it may be a good idea to find one (and learn how to use it) as soon as possible, before the government "strongly urges" you to use its "voluntary" Clipper standard.

The current favorite public key encryption program among netizens is PGP (which stands for Pretty Good Privacy). PGP is a cross-platform encryption standard that enables you to send secure messages to any other PGP user knowing only their public key (not their password).

You can download your very own copy of PGP and explore a number of other encryption-related issues where the cypherpunks hang out. (A cypherpunk is, presumably, a cyberpunk who specializes in cryptography.)

If it has anything to do with encryption, you'll find it via anonymous FTP at `soda.berkeley.edu` in the `/pub/cypherpunks/` directory. You can post your PGP public key (and download other folks' keys) in the `alt.security.keydist` newsgroup.

public access provider An organization whose resources are available for a fee to access the Internet. *See also* commercial access provider.

Public Key Encryption A security measure that enables anyone to encrypt and send a message to the owner of a particular key, but only the owner can decrypt the message. *See also* encryption.

punchdown block A device used by phone companies and network installers for connecting many wires together in one location. A common type of punchdown block has 200 contacts (50 rows, each with four contacts). You use a punchdown tool to push the wire onto the contact to complete the circuit. Wire cowboys talk about "punching in some nodes."

PVC *See* **Private Virtual Circuit**.

query A question, usually used in connection with a database language, to find a particular record or set of records in database.

queue A waiting area for messages, files, print jobs, or anything else that is being sent from one device to another. To a user on the information highway who is waiting for output from a busy server, a queue is synonymous with the rush-hour traffic that crams into the Lincoln Tunnel to get to downtown Manhattan. Managing bottlenecks in a queue is a major part of a network administrator's job.

QuicKeys Macintosh software for creating keyboard shortcuts to replace tedious and complicated procedures. With QuicKeys, you can substitute a single keystroke for a long series of commands. Especially useful for repetitive entries of the type made in interactive networking sessions. Released by CESoftware, Inc.

QuickTime An Apple technology that can incorporate text, sound, animation, and video into a single file. Despite being internally compressed, QuickTime files can become quite large and unmanageable on the Internet.

quoting To include text from a message to which you are replying. You indicate the quoted material by typing a greater-than character (>) on each line. This is an efficient and methodical way to respond to a series of questions because the questions and answers are linked.

You Can Quote Me on That

Unfortunately, the process can become complicated when many readers are quoting and posting responses to a single original statement. When carried to illogical extremes, quoting can complicate the process of discussing an issue beyond any reasonable recognition. See the excerpts below for examples of efficient and inefficient quoting.

Efficient Quoting

In his discussion of global warming, Charles mentioned that there is at least some evidence to support the idea that global warming is an increasing problem.

continues

>A report issued just last week by Greenpeace shows the steady
>rise of ocean levels along many Pacific islands as well as a
>comprehensive study of weather showing that nine of the hottest
>ten years on record were experienced over the past 15 years.

Unfortunately, Charles ignores a lot of important information that I'd like to discuss at length.

Inefficient Quoting

In Rob's response to Craig's comments about the claims Charles made, he notes:

>Craig misses the point about what Charles was saying when he
claims:
>>Charles has good reason to make his case based upon his data that:
>>>A report issued just last week by Greenpeace shows the steady
>>>rise of ocean levels along many Pacific islands as well as a
>>>comprehensive study of weather showing that nine of the
>>>hottest ten years on record were experienced over the past 15
>>>years.

TIP

RAIN Regional Access Information Network. A regional Internet provider based at the University of California at Santa Barbara. To contact, send email to `rain@rain.org`.

RAM Random Access Memory. Silicon memory that any byte can be read or written to.

ranking The order in which WAIS displays the results of a database search with the most likely possibilities at the top of the list.

RARE *See* **Reseaux Associes pour la Recherche Europeenne**.

RARP *See* **Reverse Address Resolution Protocol**.

RBOC Regional Bell Operating Company.

RCP *See* **Remote copy program**.

read To view a file on your computer screen. In directory listings, shown as an "r" next to the file name. *See also* privileges.

read notification A feature provided by many email applications that confirms that your intended recipient received and read your message. Technically, it validates that the message was opened and displayed on a computer screen by someone. You can't actually prove who saw it and if they actually read it. But unless you're paranoid, it's an adequate

instrument for putting your receiver on notice. *Compare* receipt notification.

readme A file found in an Internet host's directory that describes the computer and its service. It is one of the files that newcomers to the host are advised to download and read because the information contained is useful. There are also readme files that come bundled with personal computer software that give the latest information about installation, known bugs and incompatibilities, and product documentation errata and addenda.

receipt notification A proof-of-delivery feature provided by many email applications. When you send out a message, you can request to be notified when it has been placed in the in-basket of the intended recipient. *See also* read notification.

redundant path The secondary route that a router resorts to when a disruption occurs in the normal path it would assign for a network packet.

Reeboknet *See* **sneakernet**.

relevance feedback A method used by WAIS to arrange retrieved documents in order of predicted relevance to the criteria you supplied. The documents are scored based on the number of times keywords appear in them and are ranked from highest to lowest.

reliable An adjective that is applied to connection-oriented networks because connections are dedicated and therefore are always available. Contrasted to packet-switching networks that do not have permanent connections and therefore do not have the same level of reliability. (That is not to say that packet-switched networks are "unreliable.")

remote An adjective that describes devices or processes that are not under your direct control, as opposed to local devices that are under your control. The printer directly attached to your computer's printer port is a local printer. The printer that you connect to via a network is a remote printer. In interactions with another computer (especially a host) you may become confused about what is remote and what is local. The local host is the computer you originally logged on to. You may then telnet to another host and start another session. The second host is the remote host.

remote access Using your computer to access another computer's resources, such as programs, files and printers. You need a modem, appropriate remote access software, and a valid account. Connecting to a company computer from home, or using telnet to connect to a remote host, are examples of remote access. *See also* AppleTalk Remote Access.

remote echo *See* **echo**.

remote login To access the services of a remote computer as if you were attached to a local computer. *See also* remote, local, and telnet.

repeater A device that connects two segments of network cable, and boosts the power of incoming digital signals before passing them along. As signals pass over a line, they start to break up. A repeater amplifies the signal and reduces noise and possible errors. Repeaters operate at the Physical Layer.

reply Command that tells your email application that you want to send a message in direct response to a message you received from someone. The program takes information from the received message and creates a new header so you don't have to type one yourself.

■ ■ ■ ■ ■ ■ ■ ■ **TIP** ■ ■ ■ ■ ■ ■ ■ ■

Request for Comment (RFC) A document that contains Internet protocols, proposed standards and technical information. RFCs were started in 1969 and are identified by number; for example, rfc1178 describes choosing a name for your computer. RFCs are public domain and are available from the network information center. A directory of RFCs contains descriptions of hundreds of files. See table below for a small sampling. *See also* FYI and STD.

RFCs

RFC	Subject
1340	Assigned numbers
1250	IAB official protocol standards
1166	Internet numbers
1011	Official Internet protocols
1178	Choosing a name for your computer
894	Standard for the transmission of IP datagrams over Ethernet networks.
791	Internet Protocol
815	IP datagram reassembly algorithms
959	File Transfer Protocol
793	Transmission Control Protocol
1032	Domain administrator's guide
1033	Domain administrator's operations guide
1034	Domain names – concepts and facilities
1035	Domain names – implementation and specification
1206	FYI on Questions and Answers: Answers to commonly asked "new Internet user" questions
1207	FYI on Questions and Answers: Answers to commonly asked "experienced Internet user" questions
1058	Routing information protocol
768	User datagram protocol
1135	Trojan horse
1243	AppleTalk Management Information Base
1169	Explaining the role of GOSIP
1196	Finger user information protocol
974	Mail routing and the domain system
1148	Mapping between X.400(1988)/ISO 10021 and RFC 822

continues

continued

RFCs	
RFC	*Subject*
1341	MIME (Multipurpose Internet Mail Extensions) Mechanisms for Specifying and Describing the Format of Internet Message Bodies
1214	OSI internet management: Management Information Base
1240	OSI connection less transport services on top of UDP: Version 1
1115	Privacy enhancement for Internet electronic mail: Part III-algorithms, modes, and identifiers (Draft)
1244	Site security handbook
821	Simple Mail Transfer Protocol
1094	NFS: Network File System Protocol specification

Request for Discussion A formal proposal to start a newsgroup and begin discussion on a subject of your choice.

Reseaux Associes pour la Recherche Europeenne (RARE) A European group of research networks.

Reseaux IP Europeenne (RIPE) A group of European networks that are based on TCP/IP.

RFC *See* **Request for Comments**.

RFC 822 Describes the standard Internet format for electronic mail message headers. You may see a reference to "822 messages." Previously, 822 format was known as "733 format."

RFD *See* **Request for Discussion**.

rights *See* **privileges**.

ring topology A network of devices, or nodes, connected in a circle. Data passes from node to node: each node receives data from the node next to it and retransmits the data to the next node in the circle. The nodes act like repeaters. *See also* token ring, star topology, and bus topology.

RIP *See* **Routing Information Protocol**.

RIPE *See* **Reseaux IP Europeenne**.

RISQ A Quebec, Canada Internet. For information, send email to `turcotte@clouso.crim.ca`.

RJ Registered jack.

RJ-11 A modular jack that can hold up to three pairs of wires. This is the typical clear plastic phone jack that "clicks" into your phone at one end and the phone outlet on the wall at the other end. RJ-11 jacks are found in most homes and offices.

RJ-45 A modular jack that can hold up to four pairs of wires. This is the most common connector for unshielded twisted pair wiring (UTP) in LAN installations. It looks similar to but is larger than the typical phone jack, RJ-11.

TIP

rlogin A UNIX alternative to telnet. You can program rlogin to automatically submit your username and password to the remote terminal to avoid repetitive entries. Rlogin is not supported by every site.

TIP

rn A UNIX news reader. Available on virtually any UNIX computer that has a newsfeed.

Robert E. Kahn Designed the protocols (with Vinton G. Cerf) that formed the basis of TCP/IP.

role-playing A type of online game in which you can engage in a fantasy with other users by taking on the part of a character. *See also* Multi-User Dungeon.

ROM Read Only Memory. Chips that contain instructions "burned" into them at the factory and cannot be altered.

root The base of a hierarchical structure. In directory organization,

the root directory is the first directory and all other directories are sub-directories. In the DNS, a root domain is the highest-level domain.

rot13 When this appears in the title of an article, it means the posting has been encrypted. More of a warning than a security device, "rot13" alerts you to an item's potentially offensive contents. Works like a skull and crossbones. As far as encryption goes, it's strictly Junior G-man stuff. Convert the letters to numbers (A=1, B=2, C=3, D=guesswhat?), add 13 to the number, and then convert the numbers back to letters. Got your decoder ring?

ROTFL Rolling on the floor laughing. A common shorthand abbreviation seen in chat sessions and email messages.

Round-Trip Time (RTT) The amount of time it takes for a message to complete a circuit from you to a host on the network. You can get a good idea of lag time by sending a message to the host and noting when you get an acknowledgment.

route The path that data packets take from point of origination to final destination.

routed A version of the Routing Information Protocol that is distributed with UNIX systems.

router A device that physically connects networks into an internet and maintains network addresses. Data passing from one network to another moves through the router on its way to nodes on another network. A router using specific protocols, such as TCP/IP, determines the destination of a packet by consulting a routing table. The table provides information about destination addresses, the IP address of next router, and the network interface involved, among other items. Basically, the table tells the router where the packet is to be sent next. The latest generation of "smart" routers can make decisions about best path, fastest path, least cost path, and currently available path. The Internet is literally tied together by routers.

routine A set of instructions that may be used many times in different locations of a program.

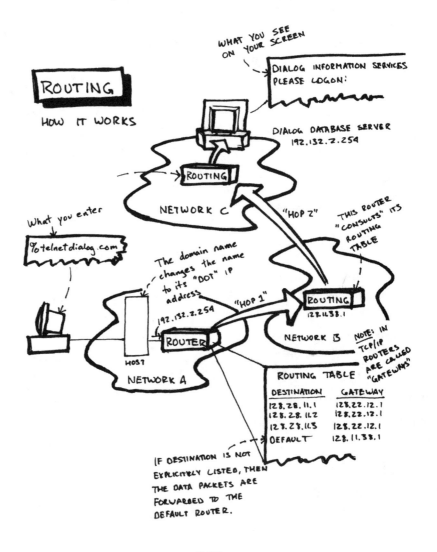

routing The process of selecting the appropriate interface and forwarding a data packet to the next router.

Routing Information Protocol (RIP) A TCP/IP protocol that defines how routers exchange information. RIP determines routes using a least-cost path method. RIP is an Interior Gateway Protocol that was taken from the Xerox Networking Systems (XNS) routing protocol. It is distributed with UNIX as part of the Berkeley Software Distribution in a program named routed. RIP is also available from Cornell University in a version called "gated."

routing table A table residing on an AppleTalk router that specifies node IDs, port status, network range, distance in hops, and destination port number. The information is used by routers to make decisions about forwarding datagrams.

Routing Table Maintenance Protocol (RTMP) An AppleTalk Transport layer protocol that defines how routers maintain the routing tables they use when routing packets on the network. RTMP specifies how routers are to exchange information to keep the tables up to date.

RPC _See_ **Remote Procedure Call**.

RS-232C The most common type of communications circuit. It's the familiar 25-pin connector that may be connecting your computer to your modem. RS-232C is a standard that defines the electrical signaling and cable connection characteristics of a serial port. The name stands for Recommended Standard number 232 version C. Established by the EIA and sometimes referred to as the "EIA interface."

RSN Real soon now. A common shorthand abbreviation seen in chat sessions and email messages, usually when referring to long-anticipated (or long-delayed) improvements, bug-fixes, new releases, or other changes in software, hardware, or procedures.

RTFM Read the "you-know-what" manual. A common shorthand abbreviation seen in chat sessions and email messages, sometimes directed in jest toward people asking questions that are obvious and easily answered with a little research, and sometimes directed maliciously to people guilty of repeatedly asking annoying questions.

RTMP _See_ **Routing Table Maintenance Protocol**.

RTT _See_ **Round-Trip Time**.

SAA *See* **Systems Application Architecture**.

screen-oriented interface A display that shows an entire screen at a time. *Contrast* line-oriented interface. *See also* character-based interface.

scroll The movement of text upward as more information is displayed at the bottom of the screen. Windows-type interfaces enable you to select a bar to scroll back or "rewind" text that was displayed earlier.

scroll-back A feature of some communications programs that enable you to view information that has scrolled past the dimensions of your video screen. Generally, this capability is found in Macintosh or Windows-type programs with graphical interfaces. There is a buffer of several pages available by using the scroll bar.

SCSI Small Computer Systems Interface. A standard established for managing the communications and connections between a personal computer and peripheral devices such as CD-ROM drives, scanners, and portable hard drives. Nearly every Macintosh features a built-in SCSI port and most PCs can be made SCSI-capable by adding a card and installing software. Pronounced "scuz-zy."

SDD *See* **Software Description Database**.

SDLC *See* **Synchronous Data Link Control**.

.sea File extension for a Macintosh self-extracting archive. Disk-Doubler, StuffIt, and CompactPro files may all sport this extension.

secondary service provider Organizations that provide direct connection to the Internet on a regional basis.

segment (Noun) 1) A length of cable in a network. A piece of cable that connects devices in a network. Segments attach to the ports of repeaters, bridges, routers, and gateways. Segments vary significantly in their carrying capacity: a segment of thick-wire cable (10base5) is effective up to 500 meters, while a segment of thin-wire coax (10base2) can only extend 185 meters before becoming ineffective.

2) The chunk of data that TCP puts together and hands off to IP to put into packets. TCP segments are normally up to 1500 bytes in size.

3) The constituent parts of a file that has been divided to reduce download time or fit conveniently onto a number of floppy disks.

(Verb) To break a file into parts.

self-extracting archive A file (or several files) that is stored in a compressed form until you open it. You do not need a decompression or extracting program to decompress a self-extracting archive. *See also* compress, decompress.

Sequenced Packet Exchange (SPX) A Novell NetWare protocol that ensures a guaranteed delivery link between workstations. SPX is a transport layer protocol.

Sequinet A Texas and Latin America Internet provider located in Texas. For information, send email to farrell@rice.edu.

Serial Line Internet Protocol (SLIP) A TCP/IP protocol for transmitting IP datagrams over serial lines such as dial-up phone lines. With SLIP, your personal computer can behave like a bona-fide Internet machine. Unfortunately, SLIP is unreliable (in the technical sense of the word) because it has no error checking capability. There are programs for the Macintosh and Intel-based PCs that provide SLIP capability. SLIP is a network layer protocol, as opposed to the Point-to-Point Protocol (PPP), which is a link layer protocol.

serial One at a time. In communications, one bit is sent at a time, sequentially, via a single electrical channel. *See also* parallel.

serial port A socket on the back of a computer where you can attach a cable to interface with a serial device (for example, a printer) that accepts data sequentially, one bit at a time, through a single channel. *Compare* parallel port.

server A specialized network device or software that provides a service to other devices. The most common services on a LAN are printer servers, file servers, and mail servers. The Internet is made up of servers. For example, the Domain Name System is handled by servers and a computer that is running WAIS is a WAIS server. The program or machine that makes use of the service is called a "client." *See also* client/server computing.

service provider A commercial, governmental, or educational organization that provides connections to the Internet. To access the Internet, both corporate and personal computers must connect to a service provider. Also known as an "access provider." *See also* commercial access provider.

Session Layer Layer five of the OSI Reference Model defines the protocols for making and maintaining a logical connection between computers.

session An exchange of communications between two nodes on a network. Individual nodes can have many sessions going at the same time. If you are printing and using email, your computer is having two sessions, one with the printer and the other with the host on which the mail program is running. The AppleTalk Session Protocol (ASP) starts, maintains, and stops sessions.

shareware A software distribution arrangement. The author makes the software freely available by uploading it to a host. You download it and try it out on your own computer. If you use the software, you send a fee to the author. Much of the software available through the Internet and other systems is shareware. *Contrast* freeware.

Stepchild of the Software World

Shareware has often carried a reputation in the computing world for being unreliable, buggy, and somewhat inferior to the standards of professionally produced software. While there's no arguing that much shareware—perhaps even the majority of it—deserves such criticism, there are still tens of thousands of great shareware programs nestled away on FTP sites across the Net, just waiting to be discovered.

A developing trend in the shareware world finds the best shareware programs being bought by software companies and converted to commercial status. Don't sit around with your thumb in your mouth while your would-be favorite shareware or freeware program is transmogrified into a commercial beast! Explore the big shareware FTP sites and be sure to *pay* the requested fees for the shareware you use.

Here are a few places to start in your search for the ultimate shareware program:

For Macintosh shareware, you can FTP to `sumex-aim.stanford.edu` and check practically any directory.

For IBM-PC shareware, you can FTP to `wuarchive.wustl.edu` and check the `/systems/ibmpc/` directory.

For Windows shareware, you can FTP to `wuarchive.wustl.edu` and check the `/systems/ibmpc/win3/` directory.

■ ■ ■ ■ ■ ■ ■ ■ ■

shell A command interpreter and programming language that enables you to interact with a host's operating system (most notably, UNIX) and run programs. There are several UNIX shells; some systems offer a choice of one or more of the following: Bourne, Korn, Bourne again, Z, C, and Tenex C. The shells differ from each other in command formats and facilities. There is also a shell for DOS on personal computers that provides DOS-phobes and inexpert users with a system of menus to display DOS commands and applications.

**shoulder
surfer**
Someone who
watches over
your shoul-
der. Possibly
it's just a
friendly
kibitzer
stopping by
to snoop and
gossip, but
it could also
be a spy who
is after your
computer
password,
telephone
access code,
or some other
piece of
information
you'd rather
keep to your-
self.

shell account A personal access set up by the system administrator for users dialing in to a UNIX system. The account consists of a user ID, password, and home directory.

shielded cable A cable whose main conductors are protected from electrical interference by a wire-mesh covering beneath the plastic insulation. (Coaxial cable is a good example of shielded cable.) The shield itself is grounded and minimizes disruption of the signal by external electrical noise. It also prevents the cable from sending out electrical signals that can disrupt television and radio signals. Additionally, in super-secure environments, the shielding thwarts unauthorized people from tapping the transmission signals. Shielded twisted-pair (STP) is an IBM implementation. *See also* twisted-pair wire.

shielded twisted-pair (STP) A type of wiring specified by IBM for Token Ring LANs. There are two varieties common in LANs. Type 1 consists of 2 pairs of #22 AWG conductors with a braided cable shield and it is intended for data communications only. Type 2 is identical to Type 1 with four twisted pairs of #22 AWG wire to enable voice, as well as data transmission.

SIG (Capitalized) *See* **Special Interest Group**.

sig (Not capitalized) Signature. Usually a reference to the signature portion of an email message.

signal-to-noise ratio In electrical engineering, a measure of the effectiveness of a communications medium. In the lingo of newsgroups and online forums, it means the proportion of meaningful content to extraneous chatter. Or as Macbeth put it: "Full of sound and fury and signifying nothing."

signature The three or four lines at the bottom of a mail message where your name and email address are shown, plus additional information if you want to insert, such as a facsimile John Hancock, a line of doggerel, or an inane smiley. Signatures over five lines are bad form. *See also* wasted bandwidth.

Simple Mail Transfer Protocol (SMTP)
The TCP/IP protocol that defines how electronic mail is exchanged between computers. SMTP describes how a system is to construct a mail message and transfer it across the Internet. It works in conjunction with the Post Office Protocol.

Simple Network Management Protocol (SNMP)
The TCP/IP protocol that defines how to manage nodes on a network. SNMP uses management programs called "agents" to monitor network traffic and store the information it collects in the Management Information Base (MIB). Management software interacts with the MIB to provide the administrator with the state of activity on the network.

Simple Wide Area Information System (SWAIS)
An interface to Wide Area Information System (WAIS) that displays sources in

numbered lists and uses VT-100 terminal emulation.

simplex One-way transmission, such as a computer sending a print job to a printer, or a satellite sending a picture to a television. *Compare* half duplex, and full duplex.

.sit File extension for a StuffIt file.

slash commands *See* **immediate commands**.

SLIP *See* **Serial Line Internet Protocol**.

SMDS *See* **Switched Multimegabit Data Service**.

SMI *See* **Structure of Management Information**.

shovelware A CD-ROM title filled with vast amounts of mostly unformatted, loose data simply shovelled onto the CD. Many shovelware titles are created from data freely available on the Internet.

shouting ONE OF THE MOST ANNOYING THINGS ON THE INTERNET is an email message or discussion group posting WRITTEN ENTIRELY IN UPPERCASE. AMONG INTERNETTERS, IT'S CALLED "SHOUTING." IT'S PROBABLY A HOLDOVER FROM THE DAYS OF MAINFRAME COMPUTERS AND LINE PRINTERS. DO US ALL A FAVOR AND TAKE OFF CAPS LOCK. Thank you. See how much quieter it is?

Smiley

Little faces you can type in your email messages and news postings to show your (or someone else's) emotions: happy : -), grumpy : - (, or weepy : -<. Smileys are also used to make sure your audience knows when you're being sarcastic. For example: "Don't pay your taxes! :-)"

Just use your imagination (and tilt your head 90 degrees counterclockwise) and you too can amuse/annoy your readers with your own cute or cryptic inventions. The electronic equivalent of putting X's and O's (hugs and kisses) at the bottom of a letter. Also called "emoticons" for emotion-icon. These creatures of the keyboard come in all sorts of variations. For a sampling, see following table.

continues

continued

Smileys

:-t	Cranky.	:-*	Pickle face.	=:-)	Mohawk.
:-\	Undecided.	:>)	Big nose.	(:)-)	Scuba diver.
:-o	Shocked!	%-)	Cross-eyed.	8:]	Gorilla.
:-&	Tongue tied.	#-)	Tied one on!	:-)X	Wears a bow tie.
:-|	Too bored to stay awake.	[:.)	On headphones.	:-)	Wears lipstick.
:-c	Bummed out.	(.:	Left-handed.	@:I	Turban wearer.
:-#	Sealed lips.	*<|:-)	Santa Claus.	8-)	Four eyes.
8-|	What next!	:-Q	Nicotine fiend.	:;-)	Middle-aged four eyes.
:-<	Sad.	:-?	Smokes pipe.	B-)	Horn-rimmed.
8-#	Dead.	:-{	Mustachioed.	:-)8	Snazzy dresser.
:-I	Hmmm.	:-%	Bearded.	:-)	Big mouth.
:-x	My lips are zipped.	(-)	Shaggy headed.	:<|	Ivy Leaguer.
:>	Shortie.	{:-)	Parts hair in middle.	+:-:	Priest.
:-p	Sticking out tongue.	{(:-)	Wears a rug.	+-(:.)	Pope.
:-9	Licking lips.	}(:-(	Wears a rug in high wind.	[:|]	Robot.
o-)	Cyclops.	%-^	Picasso.	*:o)	Bozo.

snail mail
Reference to
the U.S.
Postal Ser-
vice creeping
along at a
petty pace.
In the time
it takes you
to lick an
Elvis stamp,
paste it on
an envelope,
and put in
the mailbox,
an email
message can
cross the
country.

SMTP *See* **Simple Mail Transfer Protocol**.

SNA *See* **Systems Network Architecture**.

SNA Distribution Services (SNADS) The component of IBM's Systems Network Architecture that processes message transfers.

SNADS *See* **SNA Distribution Services**.

SNMP *See* **Simple Network Management Protocol**.

socket A subdivision of a node attached to an AppleTalk network. Each socket is reserved for a single process or application on that node. If you are printing and using an email program at the same time, there are two distinct sockets on your computer. Once a socket is reserved by a particular software process, it is not available for another process. For example, a communications program reserves a socket for receiving messages, while messages intended for some other program arrive through a different socket.

Get A Job

While thousands of people spend hours on the Internet shirking their occupational duties, you can actually look for a job (or look for an employee) online. Don't expect to breeze through the entire job search from help wanted to company car and a corner office sitting at your computer, but there are plenty of places on the Net where you can start your job search.

A few tips on job-hunting on the Net:

- Don't limit your search to computer or technology jobs—more and more companies of all types are posting openings online.

- Even though email and online communiques are typically more laid back than conventional business contacts, follow standard résumé and business letter protocols in your electronic messages.

- Check early and check often. Find out when news listings are posted and download them as soon as they go online.

- Follow the specific instructions of each posting. There's no set protocol for responding to an online job listing. Some employers will accept email application letters and résumés while others may insist on in-person applications.

For information on job listings available online, check the `biz.jobs.offered` and `misc.jobs.offered` newsgroups or use Gopher to access the online career center at `garnet.msen.com 9062`.

■■■■■■■■■■

socket client A software process that reserves a socket for a specific purpose.

socket number An 8-bit number that uniquely identifies a socket being used by a particular software process. In AppleTalk, there are 256 sockets. Numbers 0 and 255 are not used, numbers 1-127 are reserved by Apple, while numbers 128-254 are available for use by applications. A single node can allocate many sockets.

SoftPC Software that enables you to run DOS or Windows programs on your Macintosh. Developed by Insignia Solutions.

sneakernet When the million-dollar network goes down…when you just can't remember the FTP binary transfer command (bget)…when you have had enough of technology— you can always resort to the tried and true method of walking down the hall and handing your diskette to whomever you were trying to send it. Naturally,

such retrograde strategies don't work for cross-country information exchanges, but sometimes "low-tech, high-touch" is the way to go. Also called "Adidasnet," "Nikenet," or "Reeboknet."

Spam
To post an annoying (usually commercial) notice to every (or nearly every) USENET newsgroup. Spamming is heavily frowned upon by netizens and conflicts with many usage policies governing Internet practices. For more on spamming, see the sidebar "Spam-a-Go-Go".

Software Description Database (SDD) A collection of the names of files and directories found on Archie servers, including descriptions of thousands of public domain software packages and datasets.

source In WAIS terminology, a collection of files found on remote databases. There are more than 400 sources available through WAIS.

Spam-a-Go-Go

A relatively new phenomena on the Net, spamming involves posting annoying (specifically commercial) messages to several (and often all) newsgroups.

Perhaps as interesting as the practice of spamming is the origin of the term itself. One of the first uses of spam as a verb appeared in documents discussing MUDs (multi-user dungeons) and how they can be "crashed" by overloading them with useless information. The general consensus is that the term comes from a Monty Python sketch in which a group of Vikings in a diner are chanting "Spam! Spam! Spam!" while a man is forced to listen to a waitress rattle off a number of breakfast dishes with the processed lunch meat Spam as their central ingredient. (Spam, Eggs, Spam, Spam, Toast, Spam, and Spam, for example.)

For many Net users, reading multiple messages—especially advertisements—is a nuisance. Those who pay for their Internet access argue that being assaulted with "spam" postings is akin to receiving junk faxes or a collect long-distance telemarketing call.

When Arizona lawyers Canter & Siegel advertised online by spamming every single newsgroup (more than 5000 of them), they were the victims of one of the first lynch mobs in cyberspace. Reaction to the Canter & Siegel spam was so heated it made headlines in *The Wall Street Journal*. But according to *InfoWorld* magazine, Canter & Siegel received 20,000 new business leads (of which perhaps 19,000 may have actually been flames) from their spamming efforts. Canter & Siegel maintain that they're within their rights to spam, and they vow that they'll do it again.

Another infamous spam featured an ad for the infamous "thigh cream" that swept the nation, promising that the Internet-advertised thigh cream was the "super-strength original" and warning netizens to "accept no substitutes."

If you're thinking about posting a commercial message on the Net, you may consider limiting it to newsgroups (like `biz.misc`) where the message will be welcome.

▪▪▪▪▪▪▪▪▪▪

special interest group (SIG)
Email users with a common interest who exchange messages on a particular topic in an organized way.

SprintLink A worldwide Internet provider. For information, send email to `mkiser@icm1.icp.net`.

SprintNet A global data telephone network that provides local dial-up access through 600 phone numbers and In-WATS service. You can access many Internet providers through a SprintNet local number. Formerly called "Telenet," SprintNet is a packet-switching network that uses X.25 protocols. *See also* public data network.

SPX *See* **Sequenced Packet Exchange**.

SQL *See* **Structured Query Language**.

stack (verb) To type multiple commands at the prompt and thus skip over menus. For example, in Delphi, typing "mail Mail" will take you down two levels in the hierarchy of menus.

(noun) 1) Short for protocol stack.

2) A self-contained HyperCard document, called a "stack" because it consists of an electronic "stack" of "cards" that combine to tell a story, convey information, or perform a specific task.

standard A statement of minimum acceptable performance for a device or a system. *Compare* protocols.

standard disclaimer Boilerplate language occasionally seen in the signature of an email message to ward off any liability for what the writer says. Sometimes the disclaimer is to indicate the writer is not speaking for the corporation supplying the Internet connection. Disclaimers range from the nondescript: "Opinions expressed in the document are those of the author and don't necessarily reflect those of the corporation with which he/she is affiliated." to the acerbic: "Neither I nor Gigacorp presume to speak for each other." or "Opinions this informed and enlightening obviously not those of Gigacorp."

star topology A network that has a computer or hub to which all nodes are connected. The nodes are not connected to each other but only to the hub, through which all messages pass. The hub is variously called a "concentrator" or "star controller." This type of network is relatively easy to troubleshoot because you can usually find the problem in the hub. The hub is also such a configuration's vunerability: if the hub fails, the network fails—as opposed to a bus or token ring, which can continue to operate if one device fails.

start bit A logical zero ("0") preceding the transmission of a character that triggers the receiving computer's clock, alerting it to be prepared to receive the next set of bits as a character. *See also* asynchronous and stop bit.

STD A type of RFC that defines an Internet standard. The official list of Internet standards is in STD 1. *See also* FYI and RFC.

stop bit A logical one ("1") following the transmission of a character that turns off the receiving computer's clock. Terminal emulation programs enable you to select 1 or 2 stop-bits. *See also* asynchronous, and start bit.

From Our Department of Redundancy Department

Any collection of information as vast as the Internet is bound to have some repetition of resources and duplication of effort. Sometimes, this is intentional. For instance, a popular FTP site may be "mirrored" (or duplicated file-for-file) at another site to allow more people to access the files more easily.

But at other times, it's tough to imagine why some things seem to appear twice. If you're a coffee fan, consider net redundancy a good thing, and rejoice that you can read about and discuss all things relating to coffee in two newsgroups: `rec.food.drink.coffee` and `alt.coffee`.

stop word Words such as "the," "a," "over," and "up" lack value for database searches and are therefore excluded by WAIS when it searches documents. The database administrator lists more than 300 stop words. *See also* buzz words.

store-and-forward The basic concept in email technology: data is sent to an intermediate point before going to its final destination.

When you send a message, it is "stored" in a data storage area of the server. When the recipient "opens" her mail, the mail message is "forwarded" to her.

STP Shielded Twisted Pair. *See also* shielded cable.

string A group of characters or symbols used in database searches and data entry.

Structured Query Language (SQL) A language standardized by ANSI that is used in most relational database systems to search and manipulate data.

stub network A network that only transmits data between local hosts. Although a stub network can be connected to another network, it does not exchange data with them. *Compare* backbone and transit network.

StuffIt A Macintosh compression program that appeared originally as shareware developed by Raymond Lau and is now produced by Aladdin Systems. Variations are Stuffit Lite and Stuffit Deluxe. You don't need a copy of StuffIt to decompress files "stuffed" with StuffIt or its companion programs. You can download a copy of the freeware StuffIt Expander utility (which also decompresses a number of other formats and even converts files from BinHex format) via anonymous FTP at sumex-aim.stanford.edu.

sub-domain The second-highest level of addressing on the Internet. Usually the names of institutions or departments.

subnet A subdivision of a network. A subnet can be a physically independent network segment that shares a network address with other divisions of the network. A subnet is assigned a unique subnet address or number.

subnet address The subnet identifier in an IP address. In a network that is divided into subnets, the host portion of an IP address is made up of a subnet identifier and a host identifier.

subnet mask *See* **address mask**.

subnet number *See* **subnet address**.

subscribe To add your name to a mailing list, a LISTSERV list, or discussion group. You also can subscribe to online magazines like *TidBITS*. To subscribe, you normally just send an email to the appropriate address with a message in the following form: subscribe group name your name. For example, to subscribe to a fly fishing group, you enter: subscribe flyfish Mary Smith.

The procedures differ depending on what you're subscribing to, so check the details of the relevant documents for specific subscription instructions.

suite A group. Around the Internet, people don't talk about living room suites, they talk about protocol suites.

Super-TCP/NFS for Windows Windows software that provides TCP/IP for PCs. Developed by Frontier Technologies Corporation.

SURAnet A Southeastern U.S. and Caribbean Island Internet provider located in Maryland. For information, send email to info@sura.net.

SWAIS *See* **Simple Wide Area Information System**. *See also* Wide Area Information System.

Switched Multimegabit Data Service (SMDS) An emerging high-speed networking technology developed by Bell that is used in the data networks of public telephone companies.

switched access or **switched connection** A network connection that exists only for the time it is needed, as contrasted with a permanent connection that is always on call. Typically, switched connections are made through dialup. SLIP or PPP are commonly run over switched connections.

SYLK Symbolic Link. A spreadsheet and database file format used by Excel.

Synchronous Data Link Control (SDLC) A data link protocol used in IBM's SNA networks.

synchronous A method of transmission in which the clocks of both sender and receiver are synchronized and data is sent at a fixed rate in blocks. *Contrast* asynchronous.

syntax The rules that tell how to type in commands, filenames, and data.

sysop *See* **Bulletin Board System Operator**.

system administrator The person who is accountable for the efficient running and productive use of a host computer or network. Sometimes referred to as the "network administrator." Abbreviated as sysadmin or netadmin.

Sex, Drugs & Rock-n-Roll

What better illustrates the Internet's uncensored offerings and limitless freedoms than its devotion to that (un)holy trilogy of American excess: sex, drugs, and rock-n-roll?

These three topics combined probably account for more Net traffic than any other related group of interests. (However, if Barney the Dinosaur and Star Trek were somehow linked, they would undoubtedly rocket to the head of the pack.) Clearly, the Net reflects the interests of its inhabitants.

Regarding sex, there are thousands of personal ads requesting any kind of sex you can imagine (and probably a few kinds you can't imagine). Sex-oriented newsgroups range from `alt.sex.spanking` to `rec.arts.erotica`.

If it's drugs you're interested in, you'll find more relevant information in a single week of postings on the Net than a year of *High Times* and *Easy Rider* combined. Drug-oriented newsgroups range from `alt.drugs` to `clari.news.law.drugs`.

And as for rock-n-roll, there's plenty of that online, too. Whether you want album reviews, song lyrics, or guitar chords, you'll find it on the Net. Rock-n-roll-oriented newsgroups range from `alt.rock-n-roll.metal` to `rec.music.reviews`.

VIRTUAL SEX, DRUGS, AND ROCK AND ROLL

Systems Application Architecture (SAA) IBM's set of network operating procedures that enables nodes using different applications and programming languages to connect to the same network.

Systems Network Architecture IBM's set of communication protocols for networks that have an IBM mainframe computer. SNA defines protocols for data structure, formats, control of data links, and data transmission standards. IBM developed SNA to enable different types of computers to exchange data over networks using synchronous communications.

TIP

-t A flag or type specifier used in Veronica to limit a search for particular items on Gopher. For example, to have Veronica return a listing of Macintosh BinHex files with the word "tiger" in them, you type: `-t41 tiger` where the "4" flag means BinHex files, the "1" flag means directories. Some common types are shown in the following table.

Type	Description
0	File
1	Directory
3	Error
4	Macintosh BinHex file
5	DOS binary file
6	UNIX unencoded file
7	Database server
8	Telnet session
9	Binary file
T	IBM 3270 service

T-carrier *See* **T1**.

T-span *See* **T1**.

T1 In AT&T terminology, a digital carrier that transmits a DS1 (Digital Signal Level 1) signal level at 1.544 megabits per second. It has a capacity of 24 voice channels. If it uses less than 24 channels, it is called FT1 or fractional T1. Sometimes called "High-Cap," "T-span," or "T-carrier."

T3 In AT&T terminology, a digital carrier that transmits a DS-3 signal level at 44.746 megabits per second. Has a capacity of 672 voice channels.

TAC *See* **Terminal Access Controller (TAC)**.

TIP

talk UNIX command that enables two users to communicate with each other interactively at the same time. It has the same give-and-take as a telephone conversation, only you're using a keyboard rather than phones. To initiate a session, one user types: `talk user@host`

The other user (who must be logged on at the time) gets a message similar to this:

```
Message from
Talk_Daemon@bambi.cis.upenn.edu
at 15:21 ...

talk: connection requested
by
colin@BAMBI.CIS.UPENN.EDU.

talk: respond with: talk
colin@BAMBI.CIS.UPENN.EDU
```

When the second user issues the talk command, the screens for both parties split into two windows. The two parties can type at will, with each side of the dialog appearing in one of the windows. At first, both sides may be typing at the same time, but people usually sort things out.

tar 1) Tape ARchiver. A UNIX batch utility. The program takes many files and puts them into a single file for archiving. To examine a tar file named "forest," type:

```
% tar tvf forest.tar
```

To unbatch the same file, type:

```
% tar xvf forest.tar
```

2) File extension for a UNIX tar archive file.

TCP *See* **Transmission Control Protocol**.

TCP Connect/II Macintosh software that provides integrated email, Usenet newsreader, FTP, and telnet in an graphical interface. Developed by InterCon Systems Corporation.

TCP/IP *See* **Transmission Control Protocol/Internet Protocol**.

Telenet The original name of SprintNet. Not to be confused with the telnet program and protocol that is used in the Internet.

telex An international telecommunications system made up of locations with telex terminals that send and receive data. You can access telex services through commercial online service providers.

TIP

telnet 1) A TCP/IP terminal emulation protocol that enables you to logon to a remote computer and use its applications as though you were directly connected to it.

2) The UNIX command that starts the telnet program. You use telnet to connect to host computers by typing telnet host name, as shown on the next page:

```
% telnet
gopher.virginia.edu

Trying 128.143.22.36...

Connected to
minerva.acc.Virginia.EDU.

Escape character is '^]'.
```

Type the "^]" escape character to bring up the telnet command line. At the command line you can enter one of the following commands:

Command   Description

quit exits telnet
open [host name]   starts a session with the specified host
close stops the session

To connect to an IBM host, use the command tn3270.

Terminal Access Controller (TAC) A device that provides a terminal dialup connection to the Internet.

terminal emulation program
This is the software your personal computer needs to access a host and imitate a specific type of terminal. In an electronic masquerade, your computer pretends to be another type of terminal, usually a dumb terminal such as a Digital VT-100 or IBM 3270. Mainframes are set up to exchange data with terminals. Terminal emulation programs can convert your keystrokes into the control characters that the host computer expects to see.

terminal server A device that enables several modems, or terminals, to connect to a host computer by sending a single, combined signal. The modems themselves are generally stored on a modem bank.

terminal/host computing A model for how a dumb terminal interacts with a host computer. The terminal sends commands or instructions to a large computer (usually a mainframe) called a "host." The host has files, databases, and programs that you can use through a terminal or terminal emulation program running on your personal computer. But other than sending your keystrokes on to the host, the terminal does no real "work." The host does all the real computer processing. This model contrasts with client/server computing in which both client and server computers share the processing.

terminator A device attached to the end of a LAN cable to prevent signals from being transmitted on the line.

text file 1) A file that contains only characters from the ASCII character set, specifically, characters that have an ASCII value of 32 to 128. Text files of this type have no special formatting like italics, boldface, or superscripting.

2) In terms of FTP, a mode that assumes the files you will be transferring contain only ASCII characters. You set this mode in FTP with the ASCII command.

The Web Short for World-Wide Web.

TIP

The Well Whole Earth 'Lectronic Link. An Internet provider and teleconferencing system based in Sausilito, CA. For information, send email to info@well.sf.ca.us.

TIP

The World A U.S. Internet provider created by Software Tool & Die. For information, telnet to world.std.com.

TIP

THEnet A Texas and limited Mexico Internet provider located in Texas. For information, send email to info@nic.the.net.

thickwire *See* **10Base5**.

Thinnet or **thinwire** *See* **10Base2**.

thread A series of messages related to the same subject in a discussion group. With newsreaders such as trn and tin, you can read the entire thread or discard it.

throughput The amount of data transmitted and expressed as bits per second. This does not include the overhead imposed by protocols.

TidBITS A free weekly newsletter covering the Macintosh and communications that is distributed electronically.

TIP

tilde escape A type of command used in UNIX mail that enables you to issue a command when you are in the body of UNIX mail message. The tilde (~) is a rarely used character and is therefore the character that "escapes" you from the mail environment to invoke a command without actually quitting the program. To choose another editor, for example, you type:

~e

This will start your default editor. To select the vi editor, type:

~v

You can see the list of available tilde escapes by typing:

~?

Time to Live (TTL) An IP header field that shows how long a packet is to be held before being discarded. Used as a hop count. Makes you glad people don't have a TTL field.

time out Closing a connection. A computer that has sent a packet expects to get an acknowledgment from the intended destination computer when the packet is received. If there is no acknowledgment within a set period of time, the computer "times out" and either tries again or closes the connection, depending on the protocol used.

TIP

tin A Usenet newsreader that organizes messages by thread instead of by date. Uses the same commands as rn, but has an additional thread selection mode. Tin commands are mostly one letter and case-sensitive.

Tiny MUD *See* **Multi-User Dungeon**.

TLA Three Letter Acronym. *See also* EFLA.

TLAP *See* **TokenTalk Link Access Protocol**.

TN3270 A telnet version that emulates a 3270 terminal connection to an IBM mainframe.

Token Ring A type of network that connects nodes in a closed circle, or ring. Nodes pass a token, a set of bits, from one to the other continuously. To transmit data on the common cable, a node must wait until it has the token. When it gets the token, the node transmits its data and then passes the token along the circle. Token ring LANs are typical in an IBM environment. The main difference between Ethernet and Token Ring is how multiple nodes access a single channel. Ethernet nodes contend for access (via CSMA/CD), whereas nodes wait for permission (token passing).

TokenTalk An Apple product that enables AppleTalk protocols to operate on a Token Ring network.

TokenTalk Link Access Protocol (TLAP) The AppleTalk data link protocol that runs on a Token Ring network.

topology 1) A network's physical layout showing the devices and the cabling connecting them. By looking at the shape of a network, you can see the communication paths between the devices. The standard topologies for local area networks are the bus, star, and ring. *See also* bus topology, star topology, and ring topology for more information and illustrations.

2) A network's logical connections. With additional software processing, nodes can communicate logically instead of directly through physical connections.

Traditional News Group Hierarchy The seven original news groups categories established

Traditional News Group Hierarchy The seven original news groups categories established for Usenet news. There are also hundreds of so-called "alternative" news groups that were added later. *See also* Alternative News Groups Hierarchy.

Original news groups categories established for Usenet news	

Category	Topics
comp	computer science
news	the news network in general and news software
rec	hobbies
sci	scientific research
soc	social issues
talk	topical subjects
misc	issues that don't fit in the other categories

transceiver A device that transmits and receives a signal. A transceiver is the interface between a node and the network, exchanging frames over the network cable with other devices. The transceiver listens to the traffic on the network and detects contentions and collisions, depending on the protocol involved.

transit network A network that transmits data between other networks as well as between local hosts. A transit network must have paths to at least two other networks. *Compare* backbone and stub network.

Transmission Control Protocol (TCP) The part of TCP/IP that ensures that data connection is error-free, complete, and in the proper sequence. TCP corresponds to the Transport layer (4) of the OSI Reference Model.

Transmission Control Protocol / Internet Protocol (TCP/IP) A suite of protocols that work together (specifically, on the Internet) to interconnect networks and provide an array of functions. The basic TCP/IP services are: remote login, file transfer, and email. In addition, TCP/IP enables network devices to determine the physical address of LAN nodes, to map English-language names to numeric machine names, and to manage the network. The protocols were created to work with virtually any host hardware, operating system and connecting media. Networks built upon TCP/IP can continue to operate despite individual nodes being down or lines being disconnected. TCP/IP was developed under the direction of DARPA to meet the needs of the Department of Defense. *See also* Transmission Control Protocol (TCP) and Internet Protocol (IP).

Transport Layer Layer four of the OSI Reference Model defines the protocols for the control of the delivery of the message. TCP corresponds to this layer.

trn A Usenet newsreader that organizes messages by threads.

Trojan Horse A computer program that enables the disseminator of the program to access the system that interacts with the program. A Trojan Horse is different from a virus in that a virus can be duplicated thousands of times and function according to a previous set of instructions, while a Trojan Horse is designed to facilitate access and interaction between its creator and the system it "infiltrates." *See also* virus and worm.

Trumpet PC newsreader software that runs in conjunction with a Net News Transport Protocol (NNTP) news server. Available by anonymous FTP at `biochemistry.cwru.edu`.

TTFN Ta-Ta For Now. A common shorthand abbreviation seen in chat sessions and email messages.

TTL *See* **Time to Live**.

tunneling A technique that encapsulates a datagram of one protocol within a datagram of a different type of protocol. Tunneling helps to transport data across domains that use protocols not supported by the intervening network.

tuple A type of data that pairs two related values. For example, in a routing table, the two related items are a network number and the number of hops the router takes to reach the network.

TurboGopher 1) An upgraded version of gopher developed at the University of Minnesota, home of the "Golden Gophers."

2) Macintosh gopher client software. Available by anonymous FTP at `sumex-aim.stanford.edu`.

tweak To make small changes. A ham radio term applied to, among other things, software programming.

twisted-pair wire A type of wire that is made up of four to eight copper wires. Each pair of wires is twisted around each other to deflect outside electrical interference and prevent crosstalk with the other pairs. The individual wires are 18 to 24 American Wire Gauge (AWG). In the normal wiring scheme, one pair is for transmitting and one pair is for receiving. Twisted pair wiring is relatively inexpensive and easy to install and maintain. It is used in Ethernet, ARCnet and other LAN cabling. Twisted pair wiring is also used to hook up phones around a home or office.

There are two varieties: Shielded Twisted Pair (STP) and Unshielded Twisted pair (UTP). *See also* coaxial cable.

txt File extension for a text file.

Tymnet A global data network that provides local dial-up access in 1000 cities and 100 countries to online information systems such as Delphi and some Internet providers. Referred to as a "PDN" (public-data network).

U.S. Department of Defense (DoD) DoD begot ARPA, which later became DARPA, which begot ARPAnet, which begot Internet. The DoD supplied much of the vision, implementation, support, and financing for the technology and infrastructure on which the Internet is based. The original thinking at the DoD was to create a telecommunications network that could sustain heavy damage during a nuclear war or other cataclysmic conflict yet still function efficiently.

UDP *See* **User Datagram Protocol**.

UKnet A United Kingdom Internet provider. For information, send email to postmaster@uknet.ac.uk.

Ultrix A version of UNIX that runs on a VAX.

unbalanced line A transmission medium, such as coaxial cable, that contains electrically unequal wires.

UnCover A service provided by CARL that accesses and retrieves over 4,000,000 articles from 10,000 journals. After searching through the database and finding an article of interest, you can have

UnCover automatically fax it to you for a fee.

undecode A UNIX program that decodes a binary file that has been sent by email. *See also* unencode.

undirected information Data that is available to the world at large and is not intended for a specific audience. Usenet is an example of undirected information. Data that is intended for a general audience and not an individual. This is accomplished through mailing lists and LISTSERVs in which everyone can read everyone else's contributions. *Contrast* directed information.

unencode A UNIX program that encodes a binary (eight-bit) file so it can be sent by email. This must be done because Internet requires text-only (seven-bit) characters in the body of a message. A variation of this is now available for most computers. *See also* undecode.

Unicode A standard code based on 16 bits. With 65,536 possible characters, Unicode has the capacity for color and graphics and may replace ASCII (which is 7 bits, 128 characters).

■■■■■■■■ **TIP** ■■■■■■■■

Uniform Resource Locator (URL) A World-Wide Web utility. A URL works a little like a combination of an email address and FTP address to help guide users to a specific spot on the Internet where an information resource resides.

■■■■■■■■■■■■■■■■■■■■■

Universal Time Coordinated (UTC) Greenwich Mean Time.

UNIX An operating system developed originally by Bell Laboratories and expanded by others. While prevalent, UNIX is not the only operating system on the Internet (others include Digital's VMS and IBM's VM and MVS operating systems). New users are sometimes confounded by the complexities of UNIX commands and bewildered by the many varieties or "flavors" of UNIX, and the different shells, or user interfaces. One thing that seems to universally intimidate the neophyte is the fact that UNIX commands are brief and written in an obscure code. And then there is the fact that UNIX commands are case-sensitive. Even DOS

power-users get flustered by the intermittent need to use the Shift key to issue commands. Some of the flavors of UNIX are BSD and System V. Some of the shells available are Bourne, Korn, Bourne Again, Z, C, and Tenex C. The one consolation to Internet users is that most of the commands needed to scoot around the networks and manage files are the same, regardless of what brand of UNIX is involved.

UNIX-to-UNIX Copy Program (UUCP) 1) Software and a protocol that copies files from one UNIX computer to another that is connected by modem. UUCP is used by systems that do not have TCP/IP.

2) An international network that uses the UUCP protocol to exchange mail and news. This formed the basis for Usenet news.

"UUCP" plays on the fact that the copy program in UNIX is cp.

unmoderated list A mailing list on which anyone can say something about anything to everybody. (Sounds like a junior high school cafeteria, doesn't it?) Unmoderated lists are more practical than the moderated kind because they don't require the time and patience of a moderator. To some, undermoderated lists are just more American. There is some self-restraint in operation and occasional criticism from fellow list subscribers, but for the most part, unmoderated lists permit as much self-expression as computers allow. *Contrast* moderated list.

UPI United Press International. A news source for ClariNet.

upload Moving data from a local (usually smaller) computer to a remote (usually larger) computer. From the user's point of view, uploading means to send data to another computer. *Contrast* download.

upstream Usenet news flows from computer to computer. The source of the Usenet news received by your host computer is said to be upstream. *Contrast* downstream.

My Sister's Boyfriend's Mother Heard about This Guy...

Urban legends have long been a staple of the American schoolyard and office water cooler. Who hasn't heard the story about pet baby alligators being flushed down the drains of New York apartments only to grow into a colony of vicious reptiles that roam the sewers in search of wayward youths?

But according to the `alt.folklore.urban` newsgroup's Frequently Asked Questions (FAQ) file, there are common elements that urban legends share that make them more than simple stories or idle gossip.

An urban legend, the FAQ file contends, "appears mysteriously and spreads spontaneously in varying forms, contains elements of humor or horror (the horror often "punishes" someone who flouts society's conventions), makes good storytelling, and does not have to be false, although most are." Urban legends, the FAQ file contends, often may have their roots in a factual incident, but grow to legendary status in their frequent retelling.

Among those legends that the folks in the `alt.folklore.urban` newsgroup have confirmed as "100% true" are: some people sneeze when exposed to bright light; Apple Computer uses a Cray to design hardware systems, while Cray uses an Apple; a fluorescent lamp will light up when held near a high-voltage line; the term "bug" to describe a computer glitch originated when technicians discovered a moth inside an early computer; and a student once raised enough

continues

urban legend
Just as the sewers of New York City are filled with giant aligators, the electronic highways of America are teeming with rumors. These stories flour- ish for a while and then die away only to reappear months later in a slightly dif- ferent form. The most noto- rious among them are "The Modem Tax," "Craig Shergold-Brain Tumor-Get Well Cards" and "The $250 Cookie Recipe". If you haven't seen one

yet, stay tuned to your local chat or bulletin board, you'll be hearing one of these before too long.

continued

money to pay his tuition by pleading through the newspaper for one cent from everyone who read his request.

Among those legends debunked as "100% false" are: a penny dropped from the Empire State building will embed in the pavement below, the Great Wall of China can be seen with the naked eye from the moon, resorts use a special chemical in their swimming pools which turns a bright color on contact with urine, and if the entire population of China jumped up at the same time the Earth's orbit would be disturbed.

You can download a copy of the `alt.folklore.urban` FAQ file (which is copyrighted by Terry Chan) via anonymous FTP at `rtfm.mit.edu` in the `/pub/usenet/alt.folklore.urban` subdirectory. If you would like a portable, paper-based, solar-powered catalog (book) full of urban legends, check out one of the many volumes on the subject written by Jan Harold Brunvard.

■ ■ ■ ■ ■ ■ ■ ■ ■ ■ ■

URL *See* **Uniform Resource Locator**.

Usenet The mother of all electronic bulletin boards. This conferencing system encompasses more than 5000 discussion groups or newsgroups devoted to talking about specific topics. It is not part of the Internet, but can be reached through most (but not all) Internet service providers. Usenet news is so closely associated with the Internet that it might as well officially be "part of" the Internet. Managed by Usenet software, thousands of computers, including most on the Internet, can access the news groups. You read and post articles (messages) in a newsgroup. Newsreader software is required. *See also* Usenet Newsgroups.

Usenet News The flow of messages and information through Usenet.

Usenet newsgroups Usenet discussions are organized in a hierarchical structure with the name of the major group first, followed by the subgroups. Each segment is separated by a dot or period. Newsgroup titles may be pronounced with the "dots" (comp.sys.mac would be read as "comp-dot-sys-dot-Mac") or with only slight pauses to signify the obvious presence fo the dots.

There are the seven "traditional" or "core" news categories that were part of the original Usenet system. There are also hundreds more "alternative" news groups that were added later by demand. *See also* Traditional Newsgroup Hierarchcy, and Alternative Newsgroup Hierarchcy, for a listing of these groups.

User Datagram Protocol (UDP)
A protocol that applications use instead of TCP/IP to send datagrams in certain situations, such as database lookups. UDP is a connectionless service. It adds less overhead than TCP because it does not provide reliable end-to-end delivery.

user agent Technical name for a mail program.

username Same as user ID, ID, logon name, account name. It's the identifier assigned to you that is unique on your local system.

UTC *See* **Universal Time Coordinated**.

UTP Unshielded Twisted Pair. *See also* Twisted Pair, and 10BaseT.

uu, uud, uue File extensions for an uuencoded file.

UUCP *See* **UNIX-to-UNIX Copy Program**.

TIP

UUNET A worldwide Internet provider. For information, send email to `info@uunet.uu.net`.

uupc A Macintosh program that is based on the UUCP protocols. Stands for UUCP for PCs. *See also* UNIX-to-UNIX Copy Program.

v.xx modem standards Modem technical specifications defined by CCITT. The first one was designated v.22bis in 1985 and described 2400 bits-per-second modems. The others that followed:

v.32	9600 bits per second
v.32bis	14,400 bits per second
v.42	error control
v.42bis	data compression—reduces a file by as much as 75 percent

(A note for all you non-French majors, bis is the French term for "repeat" or "ditto." V.32bis is a repeat of its predecessor V.32, with some additional features. It's in French because the CCITT convenes in France.)

vapor or vaporware Software (especially an upgrade) that was promised by a manufacturer but never released. Vaporware often sounds fantastic and practically impossible on first blush, which is why it often ends up never being released—because it's practically impossible.

VAX Virtual Address Extension. A line of multiprocessing computers using a 32-bit architecture manufactured by Digital Equipment Corporation (DEC).

VAXshare The element of Digital's PATHWORKS for Macintosh software that enables a VAX to act as an AppleTalk Filing Protocol (AFP) file server and a Printer Access Protocol (PAP) print spooler.

verbose A mode of displaying full commands and messages at the system prompt in an interactive session. For example, in verbose mode, if you enter your workspace, the system prompt is "WORKSPACE>" rather than "WS>". You can toggle between verbose and brief on many systems.

VERnet A Virginia Internet provider. For information, send email to jaj@virginia.edu.

TIP

Veronica Very Easy Rodent-Oriented Net-wide Index to Computerized Archives. A handy utility that accompanies Gopher, Veronica appears as an item in a menu. When you select it, Veronica helps you search more effectively by making a keyword search of menus on Gopher servers. It then constructs a menu for you. An especially useful tool because there are 1300 Gopher sites, each with its own menu.

TIP

vi The UNIX "visual" editor that is found on most UNIX systems. vi is not as easy to use as ee, joe, or emacs; however, it is one of the oldest and most well known. To start vi, type: vi. This puts you into command mode. Everything you type is interpreted as an editing command. To actually enter text, you need to enter insert mode by typing a command such as: i. This inserts text before the cursor. To insert text after the cursor you type: a. To exit insert mode, press the Escape key.

Vines A network operating system based on UNIX and developed by Banyan. Vines stands for Virtual Network Software.

Virtual Machine (VM) An IBM mainframe operating system that supports PROFS. It is parallel to, but distinct from, Multiple Virtual System (MVS).

It's A Small Net, After All

It's funny how the Internet helps bring people together. Only on the Net, where 10 million people can share and explore any interest, passion or diversion they please, do you find a newsgroup for every interest. If not for the Internet, how would people communicate their obscure common interests from every corner of the globe?

But nothing brings people together like actually bringing them together. No matter how thrilling or engaging a mailing list or newsgroup is, it can never compare to an actual physical gathering of net-dwellers. Michael Fraase discovered this first-hand at an Internet trade show in San Jose in May, 1994.

Fraase, author of a series of *Internet Tour Guide* books, was a featured speaker at the show and was demonstrating how the exchange between participants in a newsgroup works. He decided to pick an interesting newsgroup to browse during his discussion and picked up a thread in alt.folklore.urban. This newsgroup, which discusses and debunks popular "urban legends," was considering why Levi's blue jeans had undergone a small design change in the days of the Wild West.

The newsgroup participants offered a number of theories about why a brass rivet that once bound together the crotch seams of blue jeans was removed by the manufacturer. A number of wild theories were posted online, but none of them were exactly right. One woman in the audience shouted out the real reason and suggested that Fraase post the answer.

Fraase pointed out that—in accordance with the newsgroup's ground rules—he would have to label the woman's theory as conjecture or speculation unless she could prove it. She quickly responded that she worked for Levi-Strauss, and explained that the reason the rivet was removed from Levi's jeans was because it had an annoying tendency to heat up when cowboys crouched around a campfire, which was fine until a cowboy shifted position and the hot rivet made contact with an area that's particularly sensitive—even to a cowboy.

■ ■ ■ ■ ■ ■ ■ ■ ■ ■

Virtual Memory System (VMS)
The operating system used by Digital's VAX Computers.

virtual Not physical. Exists in the software only or in the imagination of the machine. Virtual memory can be many times larger than the actual physical capacity of a computer. A virtual screen can be much larger than a physical screen.

virtual circuit A technology that makes it appear as though a circuit has a dedicated end-to-end connection, but actually many users are sharing it. Terminology used in packet-switching networks.

virus A program that can infect other systems and cause damage. Viruses are often hidden within or disguised as benign or helpful programs, often shareware programs. While many Internet site administrators scan their files for viruses, many do not or simply cannot because of the volume of files and traffic in their sites. There are a number of good freeware anti-virus programs available on the Internet. Consult your network administrator or local service provider for details on the matter. *See also* Trojan Horse and worm.

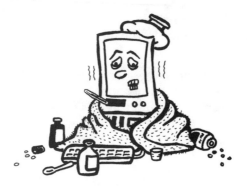

VM *See* **Virtual Machine**.

VMS *See* **Virtual Memory System**.

volume A hard disk, floppy disk, or a network file server disk that appears on the Mac desktop.

VT-100 A Digital terminal designed to connect to VAX computers. The VT-100 is a standard terminal emulation type used throughout the Internet.

WAIS *See* **Wide Area Information Server**.

WAN *See* **Wide Area Network**.

wasted bandwidth A curmudgeonly phrase, often used in exasperation, to express disdain for a pointless and verbose message or an extended signature that hogs space on transmission lines.

Westnet A Western U.S. Internet provider. For information, send email to pburns@yuma.acns.colostate.edu.

WG Working Group.

Whatis An Archie command that accesses the Software Description Database—a source of the file names and descriptions of thousands of public domain software packages and datasets.

white pages Refers informally to Internet databases of various kinds that contain information about usernames, email addresses, postal addresses, and telephone numbers. *See also* Knowbot Information Service, finger, Netfind, and whois.

Whois 1) An online database that contains information about administrators, domains, domain name servers, networks, and hosts. You can use whois in a number of ways: run the whois program on a local server; telnet to a remote server and run whois; send an email to a

wetware Cyberpunk slang for a fantasy (for now) mechanical interface device surgically implanted somewhere on the human body (preferably near the brain) for instant, high-bandwidth data transfer.

whois server; or use Knowbot Netaddress to access a whois server.

2) A Unix command.

Whois server A computer that is running the whois program and database.

TIP

Wide Area Information Server (WAIS) A client/server system that enables you, the client, to search database servers for information from more than 400 sources. WAIS uses natural language query. It also makes use of relevance feedback. Based on a search word you provide, WAIS creates a list of sources and ranks them according to the probability of being relevant. Developed by Thinking Machines Corporation, Apple Computer, and Dow Jones, WAIS is based on the Z39.50 standard for data searches. The abbreviation is pronounced "ways." *See also* stop words and buzz words.

WAIS Commands

Command	Description
###	Moves to specified number.
/sss	Searches for source sss.
=	Deselects all sources.
Enter	Performs search.
H	Displays history.
h, ?	Shows specified help.
J, ^V, ^D	Moves down one screen.
j, down arrow, ^N	Moves down one source.
K, Esc v, ^U	Moves up one screen.
k, up arrow, ^P	Moves up one source.
o	Sets and shows SWAIS options.
q	Leaves program.
s	Selects new sources.
Space, <period>	Selects current source.
^u	Removes current keywords.
v, <comma>	Views current source information.

Command	Description
w	Selects new keywords.
X, -	Removes current source permanently.

Wide Area Network (WAN) A long-distance data network that uses dedicated phone lines and/or satellites to interconnect LANs over a significant geographical area. While LANs are measured in feet, WANs are measured in miles. *See also* MANs.

wildcard A character that is used in text searches to make finding a match easier. An asterisk (*) in a character string usually means find any character or set of characters. For example, entering "*.txt" will retrieve any text file. A question mark (?) usually means find a single character. For example, entering "h?t.txt" will retrieve text files with names such as "hot.txt," "hat.txt," or "hit.txt."

WinCIM CompuServe Information Manager for Windows.

Windowed XMODEM A version of XMODEM that is faster than XMODEM, but slower than YMODEM.

Windows for Workgroups Microsoft networking software that is part of the operating system.

Winqvt/net for Windows Windows software that provides telnet, FTP and mail. Available by anonymous FTP at `wuarchive.wasutl.edu`.

WinVN for Windows Windows newsreader software that runs in conjunction with a Net News Transport Protocol (NNTP) news server. Available by anonymous FTP at `titan.ksc.nasa.gov`.

WinWAIS for Windows Windows WAIS client program. Available by anonymous FTP at `ridgisd.er.usgs.gov`.

wire pirate A person who operates illegally on networks attempting to steal passwords and access unauthorized systems and data. *See also* cracker.

wirehead An expert and experienced traveller of the Internet.

■■■

■■■■■■■■ **TIP** ■■■■■■■■

WiscNet A Wisconsin Internet provider. For information, send email to `dorl@macc.wisc.edu`.

■■■■■■■■■■■■■■■■■■■■■■

workgroup (WG) A group of users in a common business environ- ment. LANs are often organized according to workgroups.

workstation A computer on a network.

■■■■■■■■ **TIP** ■■■■■■■■

World-Wide Web (WWW or W3) A system that enables you to access documents that have been linked across the Internet via the HyperText Markup Language. Created by physicists at CERN, the particle physics laboratory in Switzerland, WWW does not use hierarchical directories or menus. Rather, the documents contain links to each other. WWW is indeed a web, connecting information from one resource to another, including Gopher and WAIS. You do not have to know the locations of particular documents and you are working with one interface— both of these aspects makes WWW user-friendly. Also called "W3."

■■■■■■■■■■■■■■■■■■■■■■

World-Wide Web Commands

Command	*Description*
<n>	Follows the specified link in the current document.
back	Returns to the previous document.
bottom	Moves to the last screen of the current document.
help	Shows help.
home	Moves directly to the initial page.
next	Follows link that occurred on previous document.
previous	Returns to prior link on previous document.
print	Prints the current document.
quit	Exits WWW.
recall	Shows a list of the documents you examined.
recall <n>	Goes to the specified (number) document.
top	Goes to the first screen of the current document.
up	Returns to the previous page of the current document.
[enter]	Moves to the next page of the current document.

World-Wide Web Browser
Nextstep software that enables you to browse the World-Wide Web by double-clicking highlighted words. Available by anonymous FTP at `info.cern.ch`.

WWW Browser for the Macintosh Macintosh WAIS client software. Available by anonymous FTP at `info.cern.ch`.

WWW or **W3** *See* **World-Wide Web**.

WYSIWYG What you see is what you get. Meaning that your computer display matches your printer's output. Uh-huh.

worm A nasty computer program that infests network environments and copies itself over and over again. Once they have a hold, worms take up more and more memory and disk space until they stop the computer cold. Worms were first described in March, 1982. The infamous Internet worm of November, 1988 replicated itself on more than 6,000 network systems around the globe. *See also* Trojan Horse and virus.

write To create or edit a file. In directory listings, shown as a "w" next to the file name. *See also* privileges.

WRT With Respect To. A common shorthand abbreviation seen in chat sessions and email messages.

WVnet A West Virginia Internet provider. For information, send email to `cc011041@wvnvm.wvnet.edu`.

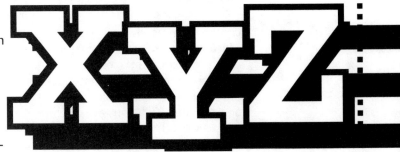

X A window system that is based on TCP/IP. A popular version is X11 which is part of M.I.T.'s Project Athena. With release two of X11, control of X passed from M.I.T. to the X Consortium.

x File extension for a SuperDisk self-extracting archives file or a More DiskSpace compressed file.

X Consortium A group of computer manufacturers that support the X standard.

X.25 A CCITT recommendation for connecting a computer to a public data network that ensures the delivery and integrity of the data. X.25 defines the connection between a DTE and a DCE. It had been the mainstay of packet-switching networks until 1991 when frame relay became the dominant standard.

X.400 The CCITT and ISO international standard for electronic message handling service. Primarily found in Europe and Canada, X.400 does not use the same conventions as the Internet; however, mail can be passed between the two systems through mail gateways.

X.500 A standard for electronic directory services recommended by CCITT and ISO. An X.500 directory is a distributed database that includes usernames, postal addresses, and telex, telephone, and FAX numbers, and other information. *See also* Knowbot.

Xerox Network System (XNS) A suite of communications protocols developed by Xerox corporation for use on Ethernet LANs. XNS is similar to TCP/IP and was used in the development of Netware's SPX/IX. XNS runs on Xerox Star computers and 4.3BSD systems.

Xerox PARC Xerox's Palo Alto Research Lab. A place of legend and wizardry unparalleled in computing history. The source of the mouse, the graphical computer screen, and Ethernet—from whence came Macintosh, Windows, and riches for many other people.

TIP

XGopher X Window Gopher client software. Requires additional software for Serial Line Interface Protocol (SLIP) connection. Available by anonymous FTP at `boombox.micro.umn.edu`.

XLibrary for the Macintosh
Macintosh software that enables you to design interfaces to network services using Serial Line Interface Protocol (SLIP). Available by anonymous FTP at `sumex-aim.stanford.edu`.

XMODEM A file transfer protocol that uses 128-byte blocks and CRC error checking. It is supported by virtually every communications package.

XMODEM 1K *See* **YMODEM**.

XMODEM block A 128-byte unit of data.

XNS *See* **Xerox Network System**.

XON/XOFF ASCII control characters numbers 17 and 19 that tell a device to pause or resume transmitting data. You can usually send these signals by pressing Control-S (pause) and Control-Q (resume).

XRemote Software that enables an XWindows user to access a network over phone lines.

■ ■ ■ ■ ■ ■ ■ **TIP** ■ ■ ■ ■ ■ ■ ■

XWAIS X Window WAIS client software. Requires additional software for Serial Line Interface Protocol (SLIP) connection. Available by anonymous FTP at `sunsite.unc.edu`.

■ ■ ■ ■ ■ ■ ■ ■ ■ ■ ■ ■ ■ ■ ■ ■ ■ ■ ■

X Windows A graphical system standard developed at M.I.T. that enables software to run on a

variety of different computers. Designed for use on UNIX workstations, XWindows has many client appliations for using with the Internet's client/server systems such as Gopher and World-Wide Web.

YAA Yet Another Acronym. A common shorthand abbreviation seen in chat sessions and email messages.

yellow pages A reference to the database of machine names and addresses that is part of the InterNIC Registration Service. The use of the word "yellow pages" is informal because it is a trademark in some countries.

YMMV Your Mileage May Vary. A common shorthand abbreviation seen in chat sessions and email messages, typically used to mean that you may experience different results from similar actions. "An ounce of the epoxy should last six months. YMMV."

YMODEM A file transfer protocol that uses 1024-byte blocks and is therefore faster than XMODEM. Sometimes referred to as "XMODEM 1K."

YMODEM Batch A version of YMODEM that enables you to transfer files in batch mode (several files at a time).

YP *See* **Yellow Pages**.

YR Yeah, right. A common shorthand abbreviation seen in chat sessions and email messages.

Z File extension for a UNIX compress program file.

z File extension for a GNU Zip compressed file.

Z39.5 The short form of "American National Standard Z39.50: Information Retrieval Service Definition and Protocol Specification for Library Applications." A standard for interconnecting computers regardless of the hardware and software. Currently, databases on the Internet are stored and accessed in a bewildering variety of ways. Z39.50 might simplify things. (Now, if they could only start by simplifying the title of the standard itself…) *See also* National Information Standards Organization.

ZIP *See* **Zone Information Protocol**.

ZIP File extension for a DOS file compressed using the PKZip utility.

ZIT *See* **Zone Information Table**.

ZMODEM The latest and fastest file transfer protocol. ZMODEM recovers from transmission errors more effectively than the other popular protocols. In addition, because ZMODEM operates in batch mode, you can download or upload several files at a time. Finally, if a transmission is interrupted halfway during a file transfer, you can log on and pick up the file transfer where it was cut off, only downloading the "last" half. With other protocols, an interruption means downloading the entire file again.

Zone Information Protocol AppleTalk protocol that routers used to exchange zone names and AppleTalk network numbers.

Zone Information Table AppleTalk router list with zone names and corresponding router port numbers.

zone A way of grouping networks in an AppleTalk internet so that a user finds it easy to find a particular network. Zones are logical, not physical groups. Usually zones are logical collections based on work groups or departments that are not necessarily in physical proximity. Zones are defined in AppleTalk routers.

zone list A list of the AppleTalk zones found in the Chooser.

zone name The designation of an AppleTalk network zone that is up to 32 characters long.

**Make the new
System 7.5
work for you!**

Guide to

System 7.5

Don Crabb The Don Crabb Macintosh Library

Guide to System 7.5

DON CRABB

Written by an industry expert, this is the
first thorough book on the new and
improved Macintosh operating system.
Readers will learn all the highlights of
the new System, including how to work
efficiently with applications.

- Intuitive, task-oriented approach
  teaches topics the way users think,
  not the way the machine thinks

- Covers all the new features of 7.5
  including PowerTalk,
  PC Exchange, and MacTCP

- Written by a world-renowned Mac expert

Covers Versions 7.5

$24.95 USA

1-56830-109-X, 350 pp., 7 3/8 x 9 1/8

Beginning - Intermediate - Advanced

Publication Date 9/94

Internet Starter Kit
for Macintosh, Second Edition

ADAM C. ENGST

This update of the national bestseller provides everything Mac users need to connect to and navigate the Internet. Readers learn how to get online, where to look for what, and how to master email, downloading, ftp sites, and more!

- Provides a non-technical approach to learning how to get connected to the Internet and what to do there
- Disk includes powerful utilities for getting online and using the Internet
- Covers news groups, email, Internet resources, USENET, and more

Covers the Internet

$29.95 USA

1-56830-111-1, 600 pp., 7 3/8 x 9 1/8

Beginning - Intermediate

Publication Date 7/94

Disk Included!

e•World: The Official Guide
for Macintosh Users

APPLE COMPUTER

Discover the next generation of online services—Apple's eWorld. Certain to be a bestseller, this authorized starter kit contains the Apple software needed to connect to eWorld. It also provides a road map of eWorld and all of its features, and is the first and best book on this exciting new service.

- Covers every aspect of eWorld, the next generation of online services
- Includes 5 free hours online to eWorld
- Everything users need to get connected and get the most out of eWorld
- The only official Apple book and software for accessing eWorld

Covers eWorld for Macintosh

$29.95 USA

1-56830-090-5, 300 pp., 7 3/8 x 9 1/8

Beginning - Intermediate - Advanced

Publication Date 8/94

Disk Included!

Everything You Wanted to Know About the Mac, Second Edition

LARRY HANSON, ET AL.

This remarkably comprehensive tome has been revised, beefed up, and improved to cover just about every Macintosh topic imaginable.

- A complete Macintosh reference covering everything from accelerator cards to zoom boxes
- Advice and answers on how to do the most with a Mac
- Comprehensive hardware and troubleshooting coverage
- More depth, more info, more stuff!

Covers Macintosh

$29.95 USA

1-56830-058-1, 1,232 pp., 7 3/8 x 9 1/8

Beginning - Intermediate - Advanced

Publication Date 10/93

The Tao of AppleScript: BMUG'S Guide to Macintosh Scripting, Second Edition

DERRICK SCHNEIDER, TIM HOLMES, & HANS HANSEN

This updated bestseller is a complete, natural introduction to AppleScript programming essentials. Readers learn how to customize applications, automate tedious tasks, and create programs without having to use a complex programming language.

- Disks contain AppleScript, many example scripts, and scripting utilities
- Progressive structure meets the needs of any Mac user, regardless of experience
- Professional instructions are mixed with practical examples for easy learning

Covers Version 1.1 for Macintosh

$29.95 USA

1-56830-115-4, 300 pp., 7 3/8 x 9 1/8

Beginning - Intermediate - Advanced

Publication Date 7/94

Disks Included!

The Word Book
for Macintosh Users

TONYA ENGST

Uniquely organized the way the user works, not the way Word works. This book gets quickly to the business of teaching the everyday things people want to do: change the text style, format different layouts, and more.

- The heart of the book is a collection of 2-page documents with callouts that tell the reader how to make text look like the samples

- Task-oriented problem solving

- Takes the reader through all facets of Word—from the essentials through graphics and style and power techniques

Covers Through Version 5.1 for Macintosh

$24.95 USA

1-56830-088-3, 600 pp., 7 3/8 x 9 1/8

Beginning - Intermediate

Publication Date 4/94

ClarisWorks Companion

BARRIE SOSINSKY

ClarisWorks is the most popular integrated package for the Mac, and Hayden reveals it for the everyday user. As a combination quick reference and tutorial, the book brings Mac users closer to success with each application—spreadsheet, word processing, communications, graphics, and database!

- Chapters cover all the essentials and provide quick, simple answers

- Includes timesaving tips and tricks

- Features discussions of special charts, QuickTime, Automated Database Entry, and the Integrated Outliner

Covers Version 2.1 for Macintosh

$14.95 USA

1-56830-083-2, 281 pp., 7 3/8 x 9 1/8

Beginning - Intermediate

Publication Date 3/94

Power Macintosh
Programming Starter Kit
TOM THOMPSON

This is the first tutorial/reference for programmers who want to enter the new world of the PowerPC. Users find all the details on the new microprocessors, the new RISC architecture, and how to write native code and emulation operations to create their own software for the Power Macintosh.

- CD-ROM includes a special version of Metroworks Code Warrior and sample code

- The all-in-one book that gets programmers the information *and* tools they need

- Programming examples reinforce explanations of code and programming tools

Covers Power Macintosh

$39.95 USA

1-56830-091-3, 350 pp., 7 3/8 x 9 1/8

Beginning - Intermediate

Publication Date 5/94

CD-ROM Included!

Virtual Playhouse for Macintosh
JONATHAN PRICE

This book/CD-ROM package explores a suite of cutting-edge and entertaining topics—animation, sound, QuickTime, 2-D and 3-D graphics, ResEdit, HyperCard, and more!

- The CD-ROM is loaded with 400M of software, enabling readers to experiment and create almost anything they can imagine

- Shows readers how to record, edit, and play back QuickTime movies; edit sounds; create graphics; edit clip art; touch-up images; and much more

- Includes demo versions of Macromedia Director, Adobe Photoshop, Premiere, and more

Covers Various Software for Macintosh

$39.95 USA

1-56830-078-6, 783 pp., 7 3/8 x 9 1/8

Beginning - Intermediate - Advanced

Publication Date 4/94

CD-ROM Included!

Design Essentials
with Adobe Illustrator &
Adobe Photoshop

LUANNE SEYMOUR COHEN, ET AL.

The illustrated guide that started a revolution within the electronic publishing market. Produced on high-grade stock with a library of full-color photos and illustrations, this is a book designers want to learn from!

- Lists the steps to over 40 high-profile techniques used by designers, photographers, and illustrators
- Provides tips and sidebars for timesaving shortcuts—and tables and charts for more advanced users
- Organized for the busy design professional with tight deadlines

Covers Illustrator 3.0 & Photoshop 2.0 for Macintosh

$39.95 USA

0-672-48538-9, 102 pp., 12 x 9

Intermediate - Advanced

Publication Date 8/92

Imaging Essentials
with Adobe Illustrator,
Adobe PhotoShop, Adobe
Dimensions & Adobe Premiere

LUANNE SEYMOUR COHEN, ET AL.

Adobe's definitive book on its entire line of imaging software and the sequel to the best-selling, critically acclaimed *Design Essentials*!

- Features the same bold format as *Design Essentials*—high-grade paper, full-color pages, and step-by-step information
- Details the latest versions of Adobe's starting line-up: Illustrator, Photoshop, Dimensions, and Premiere
- Highlights over 60 proven, Adobe-tested techniques to boost design productivity

Covers Through Illustrator 5.0, Photoshop 2.5, Dimensions 1.0 & Premiere 3.0 for Macintosh

$39.95 USA

1-56830-051-4, 118 pp., 12 x 9

Beginning - Intermediate - Advanced

Publication Date 10/93

Adobe Photoshop for Macintosh: Classroom in a Book

ADOBE PRESS

The official Adobe design seminar for Mac users—all in a book/CD-ROM set!

- With over 25 in-depth studio projects that teach readers how to be proficient with this powerful Mac graphics program
- Includes all the same materials as Adobe's licensed training seminars—for a fraction of the cost
- CD-ROM includes a library of Photoshop samples and all the images necessary for the book's studio projects

Covers Version 2.5 for Macintosh

$44.95 USA

1-56830-055-7, 210 pp., 8 1/2 x 11

Beginning - Intermediate

Publication Date 7/93

CD-ROM Included!

Adobe Illustrator for Macintosh: Classroom in a Book

ADOBE PRESS

A self-paced seminar straight from the Macintosh program's designers—developed for individual learning!

- 25 separate, in-depth studio projects teach tasks in a very hands-on format
- Features the same training materials Adobe uses in seminars costing hundreds more
- CD-ROM features sample art and electronic images needed to complete the unique studio projects

Covers Version 5.0 for Macintosh

$44.95 USA

1-56830-056-5, 320 pp., 8 1/2 x 11

Beginning - Intermediate

Publication Date 2/94

CD-ROM Included!

FAX Order Form 800•448•3804
or Call Toll-Free 1•800•428•5331

Office Use Only

Date   Taken By

MacMillan Computer Publishing
201 W. 103rd Street
Indianapolis, IN 46290
1-800-428-5331
FAX 800-448-3804

Order Number

Credit Card	☐ Visa ☐ MC ☐ AMEX	**Acct. #**	**Exp. Date**

Bill To: Ship To:

_____   _____

_____   _____

_____   _____

City   State   Zip   City   State   Zip

If We Have Any Questions Who Should We Contact?

Contact   **Dept. #**   **Shipping Instructions**

Contact Phone   **Contact FAX**   **P.O. Box**

QTY	Title(s)	ISBN	Price	Total

Products are shipped UPS, unless otherwise requested.

Hayden Books

Shipping & Handling	_____
Sales Tax	_____
Total	_____

	Author(s)	Price	ISBN
101 Uses for a Dead Computer	Mat Wahlstrom	$7.95 USA	0-672-48540-0
The 9-to-5 Mac	Steven A. Schwartz	$29.95 USA	0-672-48515-X
Adobe Illustrator for Macintosh: Classroom in a Book	Adobe Press	$44.95 USA	1-56830-056-5
Adobe Illustrator for Windows: Classroom in a Book	Adobe Press	$44.95 USA	1-56830-053-0
Adobe Photoshop for Macintosh: Classroom in a Book	Adobe Press	$44.95 USA	1-56830-055-7
Adobe Photoshop for Windows: Classroom in a Book	Adobe Press	$44.95 USA	1-56830-054-9
Adobe Premiere for Macintosh: Classroom in a Book	Adobe Press	$44.95 USA	1-56830-052-2
Beyond Paper: The Official Guide to Adobe Acrobat	Patrick Ames	$16.95 USA	1-56830-050-6
ClarisWorks Companion	Barrie Sosinsky	$14.95 USA	1-56830-083-2
The Color Mac: Design Production Techniques	Marc Miller & Randy Zaucha	$39.95 USA	0-672-30025-7
The Computer Curmudgeon	Guy Kawasaki	$16.95 USA	1-56830-013-1
Cool Mac After Dark	Ross Scott Rubin	$19.95 USA	0-672-48529-X
Cool Mac Animation, Second Edition	Sean Wagstaff	$19.95 USA	1-56830-068-9
Cool Mac Clip Art Plus!	Tony Reveaux	$24.95 USA	0-672-48551-6
Cool Mac Games Plus!	Cameron Crotty	$24.95 USA	0-672-48552-4
Cool Mac QuickTime	Steve Sanz	$19.95 USA	0-672-48532-X
Cool Mac Sounds, Second Edition	Craig O'Donnell	$24.95 USA	1-56830-067-0
Design Essentials with Adobe Illustrator and Adobe Photoshop, Second Edition	Luanne Cohen, et al.	$39.95 USA	1-56830-093-X
Desperately Seeking Solutions	Erica Kerwien	$29.95 USA	1-56830-009-3
e•World: The Official Guide for Macintosh Users	Cary Lu	$29.95 USA	1-56830-090-5
Everything You Wanted to Know About the Mac, Second Edition	Larry Hanson, et al.	$29.95 USA	1-56830-058-1
Guide to the Macintosh Underground	Bob LeVitus & Michael Fraase	$19.95 USA	0-672-48549-4
Hayden's PowerBook Power Book, Second Edition	Raines Cohen & Ross Scott Rubin	$24.95 USA	1-56830-057-3
Illustration Techniques with Adobe Illustrator for Windows	Linda Miles & Betty Wilson	$39.95 USA	0-672-30205-5
Imaging Essentials with Adobe Illustrator, Adobe Photoshop, Adobe Dimensions and Adobe Premiere	Luanne Seymour Cohen, et al.	$39.95 USA	1-56830-051-4
In Concert with Excel and Word for the Mac	Dan Shafer	$34.95 USA	0-672-48550-8
Internet Explorer Kit for Macintosh	Adam C. Engst & William Dickson	$29.95 USA	1-56830-089-1
Internet Starter Kit for Macintosh, Second Edition	Adam C. Engst	$29.95 USA	1-56830-111-1
Internet Starter Kit for Macintosh	Adam C. Engst	$29.95 USA	1-56830-064-6
Internet Starter Kit for Windows	Adam C. Engst, et al.	$29.95 USA	1-56830-094-8
Live Wired: A Guide to Networking Macs	Jim Anders	$29.95 USA	1-56830-015-8
Mac Power Toolkit	Maria Langer	$34.95 USA	1-56830-002-6
Macromedia Director Design Guide	Lee Swearingen & Cathy Clarke	$34.95 USA	1-56830-062-X
The Mac User's PC/The PC User's Mac	Elaine Marmel	$24.95 USA	0-672-48545-1

	Author(s)	Price	ISBN
Macintosh 3-D Workshop	Sean Wagstaff	$39.95 USA	1-56830-061-1
net.speak: The Internet Dictionary	Hayden Development Group	$15.00 USA	1-56830-095-6
PageMaker Design Techniques for Windows	Michael J. Nolan, et al.	$24.95 USA	1-56830-022-0
Macintosh First Aid Kit	Erica Kerwien	$19.95 USA	1-56830-063-8
The Macintosh Joker	Owen Linzmayer	$19.95 USA	1-56830-079-4
Macintosh Multimedia Workshop	Michael Murie	$39.95 USA	1-56830-018-2
Macs for Morons	Christian Boyce	$12.95 USA	1-56830-077-8
PageMaker 5 Expert Techniques for Macintosh	Michael J. Nolan	$34.95 USA	1-56830-017-4
PostScript Screening: Adobe Accurate Screens	Peter Fink	$24.95 USA	0-672-48544-3
Power Macintosh Programming Starter Kit	Tom Thompson	$39.95 USA	1-56830-091-3
The Quark XTensions Book	Sal Soghoian	$29.95 USA	1-56830-069-7
QuarkXPress Design Techniques for Macintosh	Scott Cook & Michael Nolan	$24.95 USA	1-56830-021-2
QuickTime Handbook	David Drucker & Michael Murie	$34.95 USA	0-672-48533-8
The ResEdit All Night Diner	David Ciskowski	$24.95 USA	1-56830-024-7
Stop Stealing Sheep & find out how type works	Erik Spiekermann & E.M. Ginger	$19.95 USA	0-672-48543-5
The Tao of AppleScript: BMUG's Guide to Macintosh Scripting	Derrick Schneider, et al.	$24.95 USA	1-56830-075-1
Virtual Playhouse for Macintosh	Jonathan Price	$39.95 USA	1-56830-078-6
The Word Book for Macintosh Users	Tonya Engst	$24.95 USA	1-56830-088-3
Yakety Mac: The Telecom Tome	Ross Scott Rubin	$34.95 USA	0-672-48548-6
Your Mac Can Do That!	Christian Boyce	$24.95 USA	0-672-48531-1

UPCOMING TITLES

	Author(s)	Price	ISBN
Adobe Photoshop 3 User's Handbook	Hayden Development Group	$29.95 USA	1-56830-112-X
The Complete Color Glossary	Thad McIlroy, et al.	$19.95 USA	1-56830-096-4
The Complete Trapping Guide	Brian Lawler	$19.95 USA	1-56830-098-0
Cool Mac Stacks, Second Edition	David Drucker	$19.95 USA	1-56830-066-2
The Excel Book for Macintosh Users	Charles Seiter	$24.95 USA	1-56830-086-7
The FileMaker Pro Book for Macintosh Users	Hayden Development Group	$24.95 USA	1-56830-087-5
Integrated Design Solutions with PageMaker, Adobe Photoshop and Adobe Illustrator	Clay Andres	$29.95 USA	1-56830-114-6
Macintosh Digital Photography	George Wedding	$49.95 USA	1-56830-076-X
Macintosh Multimedia Workshop, Second Edition	Michael D. Murie	$39.95 USA	1-56830-113-8
Guide to System 7.5	Don Crabb	$24.95 USA	1-56830-109-X
The Word 6 Book for Macintosh Users	Tonya Engst	$24.95 USA	1-56830-110-3

For more information, call Hayden Books at 1-800-428-5331!